COVID-19
and the
CHURCH

COVID-19
and the
CHURCH

Was the Christian Church the Intended Target or… Simply Collateral Damage?

FRANK and ANNESE JACKSON

COVID-19 and the CHURCH

*Was the Church the Intended Target...
or Simply Collateral Damage?*

Book Cover Design, Frank Jackson
Book Cover Artwork, Alero Rebekah Jackson
Interior Layout Design, Frank Jackson
Interior Layout Assistant, Olivia E. Jackson
Editor-in-Chief, Annese Elizabeth Jackson
Illustrations, Alero Rebekah Jackson

First Edition 2020
ISBN: 978-0-9968812-4-1
Library of Congress Control Number: 2020912027

For information about bulk order special discounts send your request to:

contact@ucwministries.org

Every effort has been made to make sure this book is as precise as possible. However, there may be mistakes, both typographical and in content. While the authors have taken every precaution to provide accurate information at the time of publication, neither the publisher nor the authors assumes any liability for errors, or for changes that occur after publication. The authors and publisher shall have neither liability nor responsibility to any person or entity with respect to any loss or damage caused, or alleged to have been caused, directly or indirectly, by the information contained in this book.

No part of this book may be used or reproduced in any manner whatsoever without the express written permission of the authors.

Published in Chicago, Illinois USA
Printed In the United States of America
Copyright © 2020 Xavier Publishing House

All Rights Reserved.

XAVIER PUBLISHING HOUSE

PREFACE — NOTE TO THE READER

This book comes during one of life's greatest attacks against global humanity. The Coronavirus Pandemic has wreaked havoc upon the world, as we are writing this book about it. Even as we are writing, we're also doing something that we've never even dreamed of doing before. We're sheltering-at-home.

Sadly, nearly all of the world has experienced unprecedented volumes of deaths. World leaders are discovering, that anyone can be a victim... including those who attend church, and pray regularly. Enormous numbers of church members and church leaders have already lost their lives to the COVID.

Frightened church members pose questions to their leaders, and to one another. They ask— *"How can this be?"* They begin to wonder, *"Is the church being punished?"*

The purpose of this book is not to criticize the church, or its leaders. Clearly, for those of you who have read our Bestselling Book, "THUG PREACHERS," you already know our feelings on that subject. Furthermore, we're not trying to force our sacred, and theological beliefs upon our readers.

Because, so many religious groups and Christian denominations have varying perspectives regarding the coronavirus matter, we're not sure if any of their questions will ever be "satisfactorily" answered.

Our sole purpose here is to explain viruses and pandemics, and what the Bible has to say about them. We will also cover God's judgment in the Bible and how we can remain safe, while millions are dying around us.

Because we are a married couple writing a book together, you will often notice that we will (both) speak in the first person singular, and plural. And, it may be hard for you to figure out which one of us is speaking at a given point in the book, and we understand that. With the way we finish each other's sentences when we're talking to one another, it's sometimes even hard for us to figure out which one of us talking.

However, which one of us is talking at any point in the book is far less significant than what is actually being said. Especially since we both agree on the content here.

"COVID-19 and the CHURCH" is an easy read. We hope you will enjoy it.

WARNING — DISCLAIMER

This book only provides general information on pandemic viruses. Here, we talk about the new novel coronavirus, and how it has impacted our world; in particular the Christian church.

It is presented with the understanding that neither the publisher nor authors are engaged in rendering psychological, counseling, legal, scientific, medical, statistics, or any other professional services through this book.

The publisher and authors realize that dealing with the aftermath of any form of disaster, whether natural or otherwise, can vary from one individual to another. If counseling, psychological, legal or other expert assistance is required, the services of a competent professional should be sought.

It is not the intent of the author to duplicate the information that is already available to authors and publishers, but rather to compliment, amplify and supplement other such data. You are encouraged to research and read the information covered in this book, and tailor the information to your own individual needs.

No parts or sections of this book may be reproduced in any form, stored in any type of retrieval system or transmitted in any form by any means including but not exclusively electronic, mechanical, photocopy, recording or any other form without prior written permission of the authors/publisher, except as allowed by the United States of America Copyright laws.

— **SPECIAL THANKS** —

Generally, only one name appears on the book, even though many individuals are responsible for its' inspiration, content and conception. Of course in this case where there are two authors working cohesively together to produce a final product, both names will generally appear on the front cover.

However, rarely reflects the hard work of the many people involved in taking a book from a thought to full fruition. Success is not measured by one or two people working alone. True success is often the product of many hours of absolute selflessness on the part of a team of purpose-driven individuals.

Undeniably, because I am involved in so many things, working side-by-side with me on any project can be tough. So, let me start out by expressing my appreciation for my own husband and co-author, Bishop Frank Jackson for bringing his bestselling author skills to the writing of this book. Frank is one of the most tenacious and dedicated authors I know. Any author or aspiring writer can gain so much from working with him. I'm blessed to be able to work with him at will.

A huge "thank you" to my daughter, Alero Rebekah (Bekah) Jackson for her artistic illustrations throughout this book. It was a joy being able to give Bekah an idea that we had in mind, and to watch as she breathed visual life into our (sometimes) preposterous ideas.

Finally, we are deeply indebted to the vast array of experts, clinical professionals, scientists, college and university professors, journalists, legislators, clergymen, Christian educators, scholars, orators and authors (both past and present) throughout North America and from around the world, who all played a significant role in our extensive research while writing "COVID-19 and the CHURCH."

Annese Jackson, Author

— DEDICATION —

We humbly dedicate this book to the Hundreds of thousand of brave men and women who stood up to the New Novel Coronavirus while the rest of the world, in obedience to executive orders, sheltered in place... safe in their homes.

To those of you, who voluntarily chose to risk your own personal safety to protect, to serve, to treat, and to save us. Without you, there are so many of us, who might not be alive to raise our children, to run our country... "or to write this book."

Thank you for all that you do every day. Thank you for allowing God to use you at a very dismal moment in the history of our world. And, thank you for putting your own life on the line for a total stranger. Hopefully, because of you the world is no longer a stranger... but a brother, a sister or a friend.

Now as we dedicate this book to you... may the God of faith, hope and love protect, keep and bless you for your immense courage, and for your demonstration of selflessness.

On behalf of the authors, the publisher, the editors, the associates, and all of us here at Xavier Publishing House and the United Council of World Ministries, we absolutely and sincerely "need" you to know—

From the bottom of our hearts we...

"Thank you!"

Table of Contents

PREFACE - Note to the Reader	06
WARNING - Disclaimer	08
SPECIAL THANKS	10
DEDICATION	13

Chapters

1	WHEN BAD THINGS HAPPEN TO GOOD PEOPLE	19
2	HAVE RELIGIOUS PEOPLE ANGERED GOD?	29
3	WHEN OUR CHURCH IDOLS FALL	41
4	IS THE CHURCH COLLATERAL DAMAGE?	49
5	MAKING SENSE OF PANDEMIC VIRUSES	59
6	WHY GOD ALLOWS PANDEMIC DISEASES	73
7	3-REASONS WHY THE QUARANTINE IS BIBLICAL	83
8	PUBLIC ENEMY #1— HUMANS!	95
9	WHEN TWO MAJOR FORCES COLLIDE	103
10	"NECESSITY" IS THE MOTHER OF INVENTION	115

WHY WE WROTE THIS BOOK	119
ABOUT THE AUTHORS	120
APPENDIX	124
RESOURCES	132
INDEX	136

"Our hearts mourn and weep with the family of Mr. George Floyd... and with all of the many families who have lost a loved one to police violence and racial injustice in America... and around the world."

Frank and Annese Jackson

"Yea, though I walk through the valley of the shadow of death, I will fear no evil; for thou art with me; thy rod and thy staff they comfort me."

Psalms 23:4 (KJV)

Chapter One

When Bad Things Happen To Good People

"We Don't Always Get What We Deserve!"

When bad things happen, many people fail to understand the "what and why." More recently, people worldwide are wondering why so many good people have been struck down by the new novel coronavirus. It's pretty easy to see why the world would classify the coronavirus as a bad thing. Its code name (COVID-19) simply indicates a coronavirus that began in the year, 2019.

People are wanting to know why good people are dying right along with the bad. As of the writing of this book there are perhaps, very few nations in the world that remain unaffected by the coronavirus.

The virus is alleged to have originated in Wuhan, the sprawling capital of Central China's Hubei province. But, since there have been several unconfirmed theories and suspicions on how the virus actually began, it would be irresponsible on our part to attempt to address the origin of the coronavirus in this book.

Human Suffering Is Often Based On Perception—

Whether the sufferer is an individual or a group of individuals, what suffering looks or feels like is often based on one's personal opinion, feelings and biases, rather than on research and facts.

Case in point; I'm sure we've all heard a very obese individual openly announce, "I'm starving!" Now, this isn't meant to insult anyone of excessive weight, but many largely obese people could easily survive for up to a month on water alone, unless they suffer from a preexisting sickness or disease.

In which case, the illness is more likely to be the cause of death, rather than starvation. To make a point, we all know what starvation looks like. If you haven't traveled into famine-stricken countries as I have, you've seen what it looks like on TV. Believe it! Where there is widespread starvation, bones protrude through the skin, eyes bulge... and people die.

In fact, at just one of many camps in Ethiopia, East Africa, while I was there the death count was over one hundred (100) men, women and children per day. Not from a COVID, but from hunger. So, when these people say they're starving, the meaning is quite different.

Human suffering is all about an individual's background, experiences and personal perception. Clearly, this was a famine affecting East Africa.

This is why I cringe when I hear Americans confuse, themselves wanting to eat a second or third meal for the day, with starvation.

Even the way we tend to categorize "physical and mental" suffering is blurred, because rarely does one come without the other. Often, when our minds hurt... our bodies hurt. And, when our bodies hurt, our minds are affected. Physical and mental suffering generally come as an inseparable set of misery. The coronavirus brought the whole set.

During the coronavirus pandemic, the age-old question has resurfaced again and again, *"Why do good people suffer?"* The question... in and of itself, seems to be an implied insinuation that suffering should be reserved for those who are perceived to be bad.

When the secular world talks about good or bad people, they are often basing their opinion of "good" on the idea of a person's ability (or inability) to show compassion and understanding toward others.

On the other hand, when church people talk about good people, (by-in-large) they bias their perception of "good" on an individual's dedication to the church and the person's confession of faith in God.

Researchers Point To An "Empathy Switch" In People—

Empathy, which is the ability to put ourselves in someone else's position, is crucial to our spiritual and social development. Lack of empathy was long thought to be a primary trait of psychopathy. Abusive mates are believed to possess psychopathic tendencies... with no "empathy filter."

But, research in recent years has pointed to the idea of an empathy "switch." Which means a person has the ability to turn empathy on and off. However, just because individuals have the power to empathize at will, doesn't mean they care enough to actually do it.

As humans, when we feel pain or experience suffering at the level of a pandemic, it's natural to want to understand why. Scientists, researchers, medical professionals; even laymen, have committed themselves to searching out the source of the deadly COVID strike... and a way to halt and cure it.

The truth is, that it isn't reasonable to conclude that a (perceived) good person will only experience good things... and only a bad person will have bad things happen to them. This line of thinking is very disturbing to some, and extremely tough for untrained minds to process.

The commonly used phrase..."*You get what you deserve*" is a longstanding universal belief. According to the Macmillan Dictionary, this phrase suggests, "*to be correctly punished for your mistakes or bad behavior*"—but this isn't always the case. All suffering isn't necessarily punishment.

Here again, we entertain the notion that suffering is the scales of justice by which bad behavior is weighed and measured. Consequently, people say things like "*I don't feel sorry for him.*" Or, "*She got just what she deserved!*" There are many people who believe that those who go through suffering, do so because of something they've done wrong.

Job Certainly Didn't Deserve What He Got—

It isn't easy for most people to understand suffering without fault. The Bible story of Job showcases the epitome of suffering while living righteously for the Lord.

CHAPTER 1
WHEN BAD THINGS HAPPEN TO GOOD PEOPLE

When those who are considered to be good go through trials, tribulations, and major illnesses, we want to know why. We surmise, if suffering is punishment, then why should the good and righteous be affected by epidemics and pandemics?

The Book of Job is a classic example of why and how bad things can sometimes happen to good people. When we're first introduced to Job, we see a good man who has been blessed with prosperity. It seems that Job has it all. He has an abundance of wealth, he has wisdom, and he has a great family.

"He was, in fact, the richest person in that entire area (the east)." Job 1:3 (NLT)

To his own bewilderment, Job lost his seven (7) sons, his three (3) daughters, his home… and all of his great wealth— in Just one day! That's a hard blow for the best of us.

While I love the example that Job represents in this story, I'm not sure if I know of any believers who can handle this much disappointment and tremendous grief in a single day.

Job's initial reaction to this disaster was one that we would not normally expect. Here's how the Bible puts it in the first chapter of the book of Job:

"Then Job arose, and rent his mantle, and shaved his head, and fell down upon the ground, and worshiped, Job shaved his head and said, "Naked came I out of my mother's womb, and naked shall I return thither: the Lord gave, and the Lord hath taken away; blessed be the name of the Lord." Job 1:20-21 (KJV)

Not long after Job found himself so afflicted that his three (3) friends who came to see about him didn't recognize him. It was seven (7) days before they even spoke to him.

> *"Then they sat down with him on the ground for seven days and seven nights, yet no one spoke a word to him, for they saw that his pain was very great."*
>
> Job 2:13 (NASB)

Job sought to discover why nearly everything that he valued was suddenly gone. He was left with his life, his integrity, and his wife; and even she was telling him to *"Curse God and die!"*

There are many reports of people wishing they never been born. But, what's interesting here is, Job was wishing he had died during delivery.

> *"Why did I not die at birth, and why did I not expire as I came out of the womb?"*
>
> Job 3:11

He was unaware of the conversation that took place between Satan and God that led up to his suffering. So, Job couldn't comprehend why he was suffering, but he never gave up on God.

In the Old Testament, there was always a collation between sin and suffering. The thought behind this was, if you sin… you suffer. They believed if they obeyed Him they would be blessed; if they disobeyed Him they would be cursed. It was that simple.

Job was living proof that we don't always deserve what we get. Just because someone was stricken by the coronavirus doesn't necessarily mean they are being judged by the Lord.

Sickness and suffering aren't always the result of punishment for one's transgressions. From what we see in the book of Job, bad things can very definitely happen to good people.

Humans often want easy answers to tough questions. But these answers may be more about making us feel better than actually helping us understand the world in which we live.

Just like our friends, Job's friends represented common religious thinking. They had a need for things to make sense. It gives us a false sense of control. People who sincerely have a divine connection with God are comfortable discussing their victories and their hardships with Him.

In so doing, we are able to draw nearer to Him, and to better understand Him and His presence among us, and in our individual lives. We learn to put our trust in Him alone.

"Trust in the LORD with all thine heart; and lean not unto thine own understanding. In all thy ways acknowledge him, and he shall direct thy paths."

Proverbs 3:5-6

Anyone who has been around the church for a while has heard this passage of scripture preached over and over again. Preachers love to preach about it. Singers love to sing about it and church folk everywhere love to encourage one another with it.

But, few people are really able to comprehend what these words mean until life's backlash catapults them headfirst into an ugly, dark, traumatic set of circumstances. And that's exactly what the COVID pandemic has done for the world.

A lot of us see the book of Job as a story of human suffering. But, as we read on we see the greater picture. The book of Job reveals four (4) things to us:

1. God is all-powerful and in full authority over this world, Satan and our lives.
2. Satan has to get permission from God before he can, so much as approach us.
3. God, having confidence in our diligence, allows us to endure only that which we can bear.
4. When we are willing to give up everything for God's glory, He blesses us beyond our own imaginations.

COVID-19 AND THE CHURCH
by Frank and Annese Jackson

When The Darkness Comes—

Most of us have had to deal with children who are or who were at some point, afraid of the dark. Like children, the world is showing an uneasiness and childlike fear of the pandemic darkness all around us. It's human nature to be afraid of the dark.

However, for many of us, darkness doesn't always have to mean an absence of light. Darkness can also represent the unknown, untested and uncharted road ahead of us. It's dark because we've never traveled this path before. We don't know what to expect. We can't see what's around the corner.

But, here's what I really appreciate the about darkness. It's in our darkest moments, that we see God's mighty power unleashed. In our darkest moments we are able to clearly see where we are in God.

We just read in those overwhelming words of trust that the Lord delivered to us through King Solomon. We may not know what's ahead, but we don't have to be afraid of the dark. In the dark, is where our emotional and spiritual strength are confronted and tested.

Someone once said to me, "I really think I'm a positive person. Just as long as all of my bills are paid, and I have money in the bank, and people do what I want them to do, you can't beat me being positive!"

That's not a test for a positive outlook and a good attitude. Anyone can feel strong and happy when they have no problems or opposition to confront them. But, you really can't tell how strong you are until tests and trials come.

CHAPTER 1 — WHEN BAD THINGS HAPPEN TO GOOD PEOPLE

The strength and brightness of a light's beam are not tested in the open sunshine, but in darkness. You can't tell whether or not a light is shining bright when the sun is shining strong and bright around you. It's only when the night comes or we find ourselves in a dark area that we are able to test a light's strength.

I suppose anyone can talk about how much faith they have, and how strong they are in the Lord when things are going well for them. But, the real truth is—

> *"You never know how bright your light is... until the darkness comes!"*
> Frank Jackson

"For you are still controlled by your sinful nature. You are jealous of one another and quarrel with each other. Doesn't that prove you are controlled by your sinful nature? Aren't you living like people of the world?"

1 Corinthian 3:3 (KJV)

Chapter Two

HAVE RELIGIOUS PEOPLE ANGERED GOD?

"Is God Doing A Bit Of House Cleaning?"

The thought of sickness as punishment from God has a long history. It's interesting how, so many people believe that "sickness is the direct result of the sins of the sick person or the sins of his or her relatives. During the time of Jesus' earthly presence, this was an acceptable reason for sickness. They also believed that tragedy and national disasters were sent as punishment from God for the sins of people.

It was further accepted that tragedy was sent by God as punishment for those sins." Whenever millions of humans die without a good explanation, some people rush to declare these catastrophes as God's way of executing judgment upon the wicked; even within the church.

One pastor called the coronavirus, God's Death Angel. This reasoning leads others to ask the all-important question— *"Does God really use sickness and disease to cause suffering for the sins of humanity?"*

All across America and in other regions of the world, church leaders and their members scoffed and laughed at the COVID. Comics joked about it, singers sang about it, and millions of others poked fun at the coronavirus.

Pastors defied government orders to close their church doors for just a few weeks during the pandemic. Millions of trusting parishioners were put at risk. I wondered why that was. Why would a sincere man or woman of God deliberately, and defiantly risk the lives of the members of their congregations?

I thought about that for a while. Then, I thought about how some churches have thousands of members gathered together in their impressive sanctuaries, auditoriums and stadiums for a single Sunday morning worship service. Thousands, to tens of thousands of parishioners, could easily represent hundreds of thousands of dollars per service; maybe millions.

With that thought in mind, I considered the fact that some churches hold as many as three (3) identical praise and worship services each Sunday morning. That's not including their Sunday evening or weekday services, programs and various auxiliary gatherings.

So, it stands to reason that their cause for not shutting down may not be about faith in God at all... but about dollars and cents. For some churches, the monetary losses could be great.

Since a lot of people give both spontaneously and emotionally, if they miss out on giving their financial contribution on a particular Sunday, that money is gone forever. They will continue to give when they return to church, but they may not give retroactively. Leaders understand that.

This is why many pastors were striving to prevent loss of revenue. Unfortunately, loss of life within the congregation is an incidental loss.

The Pastor's Family Dynasty Is Not The Kingdom Of God—

When Jesus called and commissioned us to build His church, the pastor's personal family business empire was not what He had in mind.

The modern church is big business these days. A lot of preachers have become extremely wealthy from the ministry. Many church leaders are millionaires, because of the ministry. Private jets, yachts, exotic cars, mansions are all a part of the family dynasty.

In my book THUG PREACHERS, I talk about how a lot of pastors have set up their church or ministry as their personal family business. In fact, the church is the only private family business I know of, where the business's owner (the pastor) and his or her family enjoy all of the lucrative benefits of absolute business ownership, at someone else's expense.

Here's how it works. The pastor builds His own empire of great wealth, but you the membership pay all of the expenses and perform all of the work of building and expanding these dynasties. Some churches exist for the sole purpose of financially supporting the pastor and his or her family.

They will make you think you're all one big happy church family. The pastor may refer to you as his or her son or daughter. You love your pastor and would do anything for him. You begin to feel like an actual member of the pastor's family.

To get you fired up to give your last dime, your last drop of blood, and to work hard they convince you that you have some pseudo-ownership in the church. They will tell you, "This isn't my church. This is our church!" If that's the case, find out who owns the church on paper.

This kind of leadership isn't new. It dates all the way back to the Old Testament. There have always been preachers who were more concerned about themselves than their flock. In the book of Isaiah, The prophet, Isaiah called them greedy dogs who had nothing worthwhile... to say to the people.

> *"All their watchmen are blind, they are unaware. All of them are like mute dogs, unable to bark. They pant, lie down, and love to snooze.*
>
> *The dogs have big appetites; they are never full. They are shepherds who have no understanding; they all go their own way, each one looking for monetary gain."*
>
> Isaiah 56:10-11 (NET)

One way you will know this is true is when only immediate family members can rise to executive leadership status. The regular members who actually paid for, and built the church will never be able to surpass a member of the church's first family... no matter how qualified that member may be. Or how unqualified the first family members may be.

CHAPTER 2 — HAVE RELIGIOUS PEOPLE ANGERED GOD?

The regular members will always bump their head on the invisible glass ceiling that is there for all non-family members. The problem with a glass ceiling is you can't see if from down below. Whenever you look up, you think, the sky is the limit. But, you would be wrong.

When the senior pastor dies, his or her family will continue to own and run their family dynasty. And, you and the other congregates will continue to pay all of the bills and, to build and expand it.

To some of you, as we write about these kinds of things in this book, we don't sound like real people of God to you... do we? But, we are able to say these things... because we ARE real people of God.

Nowhere outside of the church world, is this even remotely possible for you, or anyone to honestly and legitimately build a personal empire for you and your family, at the monetary expense of the people who work for the family—for free!

Whether in the church or in corporate America, when solid business minds stop for a moment to actually think about this kind of a deal, they are forced to realize that this really doesn't make good "business sense." Yet it continues to happen in the church across America, and around the world.

Pastors are concentrating more on building their own personal empires, than they are on building God's Kingdom. Their plan is to gather as many people together as possible. This is accomplished by way of larger buildings, multiple services, proselytizing, and modern technology.

Members, visitors and supporters represent dollars. This is how high profile preachers keep score. It's all about the number of people and the amount of money. So they welcome members of other churches to join their church.

Some of the world's biggest and most famous preachers have admittedly and deliberately made a conscious decision to side-step preaching about sin, hell, the devil and eternal damnation. They say, they don't want to offend or depress the members of their enormous congregations.

As their church attendance and membership list grow bigger and bigger, these leaders dupe the members and (often themselves) into believing that they are actively building God's Kingdom. The congregation confuses overflowing auditoriums with fishing for souls.

Church People Are Fishing In An Aquarium—

Jesus has called and appointed us to reaching out to the lost everywhere. To the serious caretaker of truth, the New Testament emphasizes Kingdom Building more than any other directive from Jesus. He said if we follow Him He would teach us to fish for lost souls.

> "And he saith unto them, Follow me, and I will make you fishers of men."
>
> Matthew 4:19 (KJV)

Take note of how excited all of the members are when they see people from other churches join their church. They really think this is what Jesus was talking about. They actually believe they are fulfilling the "Great Commission!" They call this, adding to the church.

I've always said, "If you're not fishing... you're not following!" What a lot of church folk are doing today is moving people from one church to another. This isn't Kingdom Building at all. This is the same as fishing in an aquarium.

Where Did All Of The Gospel Revivals Go?—

Whatever happened to all of the Spirit-filled gospel revivals... where dozens, to hundreds of lost souls would come to Christ in a single night? Now, this is what Kingdom Building is all about. When I first got saved, revival crusades could be found everywhere.

No respectable holiness or full-gospel church would go year after year without revivals just as churches are doing today. The revival wasn't about entertainment or "feel-good" church programs. It was about getting lost souls saved, and saved folks stronger.

In the five-fold ministry, the ministry of the evangelist is a dying art form. The five-fold ministry is a term referring to the five ministry roles of the Apostles, Prophets, Evangelists, Pastors and Teachers. It's the Biblical blueprint we are given to equip people and grow the Kingdom.

> *"So Christ himself gave the apostles, the prophets, the evangelists, the pastors and teachers, to equip his people for works of service, so that the body of Christ may be built up until we all reach unity in the faith and in the knowledge of the Son of God and become mature, attaining to the whole measure of the fullness of Christ."*
> Ephesians 4:11-13

Well, it looks like everyone heard the part about apostles, prophets and pastors, but somehow preachers seem to have missed the part about evangelists and teachers. Evangelists, like Scott Bradley (for example) in Chicago, are few and far between. The role of an evangelist is very specialized and narrowly focused.

The main responsibility of the evangelist is to win souls. His message is one of good news, hope and salvation. Pastors usually preach from all over the Bible, but the evangelist's focus is strictly Kingdom Building; nothing less.

Every day as I saw more and more reports of church leaders and church members who had died from the COVID come forth, I became concerned. I had begun to wonder if all of these church-related deaths were coincidental; and I'm sure some of them were.

The one thing I don't want to do at this time is to paint all of these church-related deaths with too broad of a brush. I'm sure that there were some absolutely wonderful brothers and sisters in the Lord who may have gotten swept up in the death wave.

Churches have gotten away from the great work that God has called us to. Real Kingdom Building is more of a thing of the past for most churches. Today's large modern churches are nothing more than watering holes for people who have come from local churches.

Let me give you an example of how this works. Years ago, we had self-sustained communities. We had whatever anyone needed. We had stores where we could obtain shoes, furniture, clothing. We had theaters, pharmacies, restaurants, medical and dental care... we even had department stores. And, we had them all right there in our neighborhoods... all within walking distance.

Then someone came up with the idea of building a mall, where all of these businesses could be housed in one space. Everything that I just named, could now be found in the malls.

Neighborhood stores began to suffer as their "bread and butter" customers started traveling to the big malls to spend their money. This resulted in the vast majority of the neighborhood businesses (like the "ma and pa" corner grocery store) shutting down due to a lack of customer support.

The same holds true in the Christian church community. Smaller neighborhood and family friendly churches were easily found in any neighborhood. Did you ever wonder why some fairly decent sized community churches were built without parking lots?

I've heard people say it was because of poor planning or design. Well actually, that isn't why. It was because the people who were served by those churches came from within the neighborhood. They didn't need parking lots. They walked to church.

As with the introduction of malls, churches began to introduce the idea of constructing larger buildings that could hold more people. Some even purchased super-sized sports arenas and stadiums that could hold tens of thousands of people.

Justifiably, they called these enormous gathering places, mega-churches. People began to leave the neighborhood churches faster than they left their local community stores and businesses.

To accommodate the exodus from the local churches, mega-churches began adding more and more services. Now, supporters can decide which one of the three (3) or more identical services they feel like attending on Sunday.

SOME CHURCHES SPREAD MORE DISEASE THAN CURE

Infectious diseases spread faster, and can travel much further than cure. It has been proven easier to spread the coronavirus than to cure it.

Disease Is Easier To Spread Than Cure—

Disease is a lot easier to spread than cure. The spreading of disease requires no special training or expertise. It doesn't require a medical degree from the Harvard School of Medicine, to be a spreader of disease. Anyone can do it.

Likewise, some churches spread more disease than cure. When pastors or the members of the congregation are insensitive or unkind to their visitors or new members... or when they practice a double standard among the members of the church, this is the same as spreading an infectious disease.

I find it interesting, how church members make a bee-line to their friends and buddies when the worship service ends. They're more excited about socializing with one another than they are about greeting visitors to their churches.

While the members are busy shaking hands with, and hugging each other, the visitor is left alone to fend for himself. Not only are you not going out to fish, but you're not even trying to reach the lost when the Lord brings them into your church and plops them right down in the pew in front of you.

When members band together with another member, or even a visitor to tear down or to destroy the pastor and his reputation, they are spreading disease. Whether the pastor or any leader or member of the church is the guilty party, it is infectious, and like any other disease, it must be stopped. When church members tell people, who are survivors of church abuse, that it was their fault, they are spreading more disease.

Because infected members of the church are highly contagious, it would be best if those who are vulnerable would avoid them. It can be dangerous to the church or ministry to have infectious and contagious individuals in positions of influence or authority.

Infected ministers, often find ways to destroy or split the church. They tend to whisper about the pastor's shortcomings and the flaws in his individual ministry. To them, his sermon is usually off point. They sometimes create and circulate rumors about the pastor, where no fault existed. They are never satisfied with the pastor's triumphs and accomplishments.

Sooner or later, the new convert or the new member finds himself caught up in this whirlwind of church discord. After a while, they begin to wonder if being in the church is worth it. They may even start to believe that there is no point in trying to live flawlessly for God, since no one else seems to be doing it.

It is the responsibility of the church to make sure that this does not happen! If a particular local church is not qualified to help these people, that church owes it to that person, to direct them to somewhere or someone who can help them.

"Many false prophets will arise and will mislead many." Matthew 24:11 (NASB)

Chapter Three

WHEN OUR CHURCH IDOLS FALL

"Why Jesus Said, "Follow Me!"

My son has a slight, but odd fear of heights but rather strangely, he's flies airplanes. I asked him how he's able to soar through the air while piloting an aircraft but is uncomfortable on a 12-foot ladder. His answer was simply, "It's just different."

He seems to think, in an aircraft he's in control, but while standing on a ladder placed against the outside of the house, the ladder could slide out from under him. He's comfortable pushing an airplane through the clouds at 10,000 feet above the earth, but he's uncomfortable standing on a ladder at just 10 feet. He doesn't seem to get the concept of "the higher you soar or the climb, the greater the fall."

He's not the only one who doesn't get it. 21st-Century church don't get it either. Modern Christian church preachers are looked upon as idols and objects of adoration, and sex symbols rather than vessels of God. And, that isn't the worse of it. The worse thing about it is they proudly and carnally welcome, encourage and enjoy this type of admiration and praise.

They rise high in the eyes of the people. They soar high like rock stars. They have become religious celebrities. But, have you ever seen what happens when major celebrities fall?

Football great, Orenthal James Simpson (the Juice) was such a star. O.J. Simpson had it all. He was the only player in the game to ever rush for over 2,000 yards in the NFL regular 14-game season. Simpson was inducted into the College Football Hall of Fame in 1983 and the Pro Football Hall of Fame in 1985.

He appeared in seventeen (17) movies and TV shows. He co-anchored 447 episodes of ESPN's Monday Night Football, and he was credited for being the subject of fifty-two (52) various other TV shows. That sounds pretty high to me. I'm sure we all know of the rise and fall of O.J. Simpson.

After being implicated as a suspect in the deaths of his ex-wife Nicole Brown Simpson and her friend Ron Goldman, Simpson's high flying spiraled into an out of control nose dive. He soon learned, the higher you rise, the greater the fall.

CHAPTER 3 — WHEN OUR CHURCH IDOLS FALL

When he fell, the only one who may have seen a bright side to his fall was perhaps, the "King of Pop" Michael Jackson. Mr. Simpson's troubles took the world's critical spotlight off of Michael Jackson who was being widely criticized at that time, for his largely known interaction with young boys. Michael may have also learned that great heights can result in hard falls.

Some of America's biggest names of televangelists joined the list of fallen personalities. The team of Jim and Tammie Faye Bakker was one of the greatest success stories in all of televangelism. Their powerful PTL Club TV show was seen around the world.

The Bakkers were where others aspire to be even now, but like secular celebrities they fell hard at the result of their alleged business practices and Jim's alleged indiscretions. They fell harder than a fallen star from the galaxies. Jim went to prison.

Although the evidence was not particularly strong, Jim Bakker was convicted in 1989 and sentenced to 45 years in prison. The sentence was later reduced to eight years, and he was released in 1994.

So, after eight (8) years and at least one (1) nervous-breakdown, Bakker was released from The Federal Bureau of Prisons custody on December 1, 1994 owing the Internal Revenue Service $6 million.

In 1992, Tammie Faye divorced Jim Bakker while he was still behind bars. She remarried one (1) year later. On July 20, 2007 Tammie Faye Messner died of lung cancer at age 65.

Other religious leaders topping the list of alleged fallen soldiers, include Jimmy Swaggert and Robert Tilton. But of course, these fews names would only represent the tip of the iceberg. Leaders who have fallen from grace aren't just at the major celebrity level, many local church leaders make the list as well.

Pentecostal preachers seem to get more backlash than others, when they fall. Perhaps because they emphasize a stronger moral position than most other Christian church leaders.

When Leaders Fall Others Are Adversely Affected—

When our church idols fall, others are affected. It doesn't matter whether it's a mega-church pastor, or a small local church preacher. It may even be a well-known Bible teacher, an acclaimed musician, or a Christian author. Adverse reactions happens.

In warfare, they call it collateral damage when innocent bystanders become victims of a bombing attack on a nation. It's pretty much the same in spiritual warfare. When religious leaders self-implode spiritually, a lot of innocent people get hurt.

So many believers who have looked to these leaders as their example, their inspiration, and the person who most helped them develop a personal relationship with Jesus. I have been on both sides of the spectrum. I have been hurt by those whom I trusted. And, I have hurt others who trusted me to be their shining example of Christian rock-solidness, but I failed them.

People were hurt by my actions. Even though many years have passed, my heart still aches today because of the hurt that I caused others. It happens all the time and at many different levels and sizes of church ministries.

"Christianity Today" reported on what they called, "a growing pile of fallen leaders." Whenever I read something like this I feel sorry for the people who are adversely affected by the actions of someone who they trusted. The noted author and therapist, Dr. Chet Welds says, "When a pastor falls into sin, the ripple effect on the lives of others is often immeasurable."

What a lot of people aren't aware of is, when there is trouble in a pastor's relationship with God, it isn't just the pastor who is adversely affected. The pastor's entire household is affected. Where there are young children involved, the impact upon the household can be even more devastating.

Every fallen Christian church or ministry leader, represents innocent victims. Sometimes the damage is earth-shaking. Other times, it may be just a faint tremor, but someone else is always affected when leaders fall. The members of the church suffer. They try to figure out their next move. Confused and bewildered, they scatter.

> *"But when he saw the multitudes, he was moved with compassion on them, because they fainted, and were scattered abroad, as sheep having no shepherd."* Matthew 9:36 (KJV)

People are left confused, wondering *"What do I do now?"* In some cases they find other churches, but their trust is broken. Then, there are the ones who begin to question whether any of this real, and sadly, they turn back to the world.

This is why Jesus said, Follow Me." He didn't say that we should follow His leaders, or His churches, or even other church members, but He Said, "Follow Me!" We are to follow our church leaders, but only as they follow Jesus Christ. No leader is above Christ.

If hurting church members can somehow see that their hurt didn't come from Jesus. It came from men and women who are not unlike themselves.

What the spiritual fallout from these fallen religious idols reveals to us is, somewhere along the way, we allowed our focus, attention and trust to transfer from our Savior over to our leaders. The Bible clearly teaches that we should look to Jesus, not man.

> *"Looking unto Jesus the author and finisher of our faith; who for the joy that was set before him endured the cross, despising the shame, and is set down at the right hand of the throne of God."* Hebrews 12:2 (KJV)

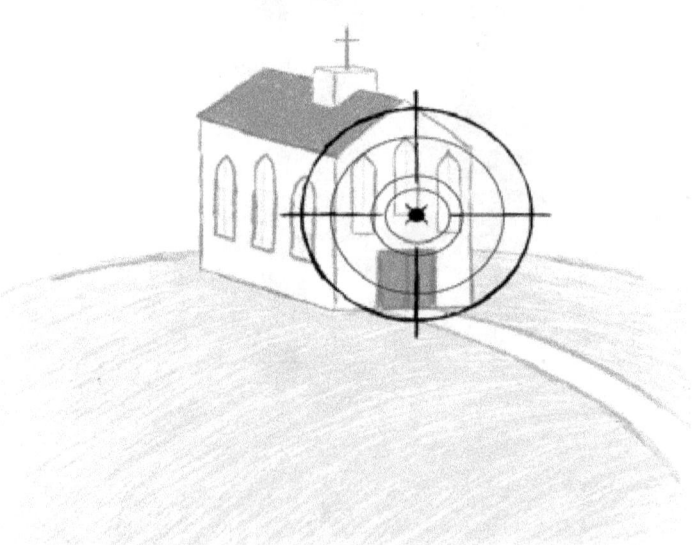

Collateral Damage:

"Any injury inflicted on something other than an intended target specifically: civilian casualties of a military operation."

Merriam Webster's Dictionary

Chapter Four

WAS THE CHURCH COLLATERAL DAMAGE?

"Was The Christian Church The Intended Target Or Part Of The Spillover Effects"

There has been much speculation as to whether or not the coronavirus was the wrath of God executing long overdue His Judgment upon the world. The confusion for many is that the church population has been just as affected by the COVID as the unchurched.

Church leaders and their members had begun dropping early in the pandemic. There's no doubt about it, the coronavirus is no respecter of person or status. Anyone is fair game. Well-established longstanding denominations were losing their state, national and international executive clergy in record numbers.

A lot of hell-fire and brimstone preachers declared that this was God killing off false prophets, and fake preachers and teachers. It was as though (so they taught) this was God's way of purging the pulpit and cleansing His church.

That may be true, but that isn't what has bothered me in all of this pandemic chaos. The thing that has troubled me the most has been the collateral damage.

Who... Or What Is Collateral Damage?—

Now, I really want to answer the question concerning the church as collateral damage, after I explain collateral damage. Let's first look at what the Merriam Webster dictionary says this term means:

> "Any injury inflicted on something other than an intended target specifically: civilian casualties of a military operation."

Simply put, according to Merriam Webster's dictionary, collateral damage is defined as damage to things that are incidental to the intended target.

Collateral Damage is Actually Very Common—

Collateral damage is more common than you might think. It isn't only about civilian casualties of war. It can also take place within our family when we've been hurt by something or someone else, no matter how long ago.

You may have struggled with feeling as though you were collateral damage at some point in your own life. Someone else may have accomplished their own goals, but at the expense of your self-esteem, self-worth emotional stability, peace of mind and personal dignity. Because if you've been hurt, you cause hurt to someone else. Or you find yourself withdrawing from a loved one.

Maybe your parent(s) forced you to eat all of your spinach, so you lash out when your child is finicky about eating the well-balanced meal you so graciously prepared for him or her. Or perhaps, because you got spanked for receiving less than perfect grades in school, your kids get spanked for not bringing home flawless report cards.

Maybe, because your parents never expressed their love to you, and their harsh negative words and stone-cold intonation pounded your fragile heart, you struggle with your own self-worth. The greater problem is, now your kids are having their tender hearts pounded just as yours was. And, you can't see it.

Sadly, you are continuing the cycle while hurting your children. So, now your children are just as abused as you were. Your child is now caught up in the spill-over effects of your horrible childhood. You try to rationalize your actions by saying, *"This is how I was raised, and I turned out just fine!"* Oh really?

The truth is, not only were you left scarred, but your children who had nothing to do with how you were treated as a child, are **"collateral damage."** Your parents may have intentionally directed their frustrations and hostilities towards you, but they have also indirectly hurt your children in the process.

At some point in your life, your trust in your mate may have been shattered when they cheated on you. But, now your faithful and dedicated spouse must pay for the sins of your previous mate, as their every move and loyalty to you is challenged.

Your past can often affect who you are. You work endlessly for the acceptance of others. And, you still fail to meet their standards of acceptance. **Sometimes you may even find yourself struggling too hard to be accepted** by a loved one or by God, who (by-the-way) loves you right where you are.

When Collateral Damage Is Greater Than The Target—

Timothy McVeigh and Terry Nichols, both ex-Army soldiers, plotted the worse homegrown terrorist attack in U.S. history. They wanted to destroy a federal symbol.

On the morning of April 19, 1995, McVeigh parked a rented Ryder truck in front of the Alfred P. Murrah Federal Building in downtown Oklahoma City. Inside the truck was an enormous man-made bomb. McVeigh exited the truck and got into his getaway car. At precisely 9:02 a.m., he detonated the bomb.

Sure they accomplished their goal of destroying a federal symbol, but at what price? The blast destroyed the entire north wall of the Murrah Federal Building (nearly half the building). Dozens of cars were incinerated and more than 300 nearby buildings were damaged or destroyed. 168 people were killed 19 children. Over 500 innocent people were injured.

During the September 11 attacks of 2001, 2,977 victims and 19 hijackers were killed and more than 6,000 others were injured. The immediate deaths included 265 on the four planes (including the terrorists), 2,606 in the World Trade Center and in the surrounding area, and 125 at the Pentagon. When earth-shaking events take place anywhere in the world, there is always collateral damage. —*It's All Collateral Damage!*

When Collateral Damage Is The Result Of Abuse Of Power—

In 1993 Alcohol, Tobacco and Firearms (ATF) agents tried to serve a search warrant at the Branch Davidian compound and their Mt. Carmel Church Headquarters in Waco, Texas.

CHAPTER 4 — IS THE CHURCH COLLATERAL DAMAGE?

Unable to serve the warrant the ATF attempted a raid. An intense gun battle erupted, leaving four (4) government agents and six (6) Branch Davidians dead.

Following the ATF's failed raid attempt on the compound, a siege was initiated by the Federal Bureau of Investigation (FBI). The total law enforcement presence was 900 officers.

After 51-days of waiting the FBI got the green light from U.S. Attorney General Janet Reno. They launched an intense tear gas attack in an attempt to force the Branch Davidians out of hiding. But, during the attack, the entire Mount Carmel Church Center (somehow) became engulfed in flames.

Within one-hour, the compound had been reduced to a pile of ashes. In the smothering ashes were the remains of 76 Branch Davidians, including 25 children, two pregnant women and David Koresh.

In another case, on 22 November 2014 Tamir Rice, a 12-year old African-American, was shot in Cleveland, Ohio by CPD officer Timothy Loehmann. A 911-caller saw young Tamir playing alone in a neighborhood park. He reported that the child had a gun. The caller even said, *"It may not be real."*

When police arrived on the scene, (in the video) you can see falling to the ground within a second or two of officer Loehmann exiting his police cruiser. The officer had already fired two rounds into a 12-year old child, who was playing alone with a toy.

In fairness to both of the responding officers, they may have very well have feared for their lives. But, their fear would have been the result of other young men in urban America who do carry and point real weapons at people.

Tamir was playing with a toy weapon. Looking back, we all know that now. But, the officers (allegedly) didn't believe they had time to figure it out then.

Could this have been handled differently, is the question that the community has asked over and over. The obvious answer is yes! It could have been, and it has been handled differently in thousands of other cases. They were in a situation where they felt they needed to act quickly. Should experienced officers have put themselves in such a situation, in the first place?

This isn't the first time that these two officers have had to respond to a weapons call. They could have taken just as much time in approaching the suspect, as they have in other responses. This would have given them the time needed to confirm if this was a toy gun, as the caller suggested it might be.

Generally, officers don't pull directly up to (within a few feet) a gun-wielding suspect. They are trained to stop the vehicle at a safe distance. Then they exit the vehicle while using the vehicle as a shield or a protective barrier between them and the perceived danger. Then, they call out orders to the suspect, starting with... "Show me your hands!"

Trained law enforcement agents realize that any threats from the suspect will most likely happen with the suspect's hands. So naturally, they will want to see the hands. The Secret Service and executive security agents are trained to constantly pay attention to the hands of individuals. If anyone in a crowd raises suspicions, agents immediately look towards the person's hands.

CHAPTER 4 — IS THE CHURCH COLLATERAL DAMAGE?

The CPD officers who approached and shot Tamir Rice were both trained to maintain a safe distance until the suspect was on the ground with his weapon visible and away from his body. At that point, one officer would approach the suspect while the other officer held his service weapon trained on the suspect until he was clearly handcuffed and in police custody.

In Cleveland, Ohio the life of an innocent young child was snuffed out. While in Waco Texas, twenty-five (25) young and innocent children were killed because of, what might have been the poor judgment on the part of others. The actual number of children dead is twenty-seven (27) if (like me) you count the two unborn babies who were still nestled away in their mothers' wombs.

—It's All Collateral Damage!

When Collateral Damage Is The Result Civilian Power—

In the corporate world, and the political world alike, it isn't uncommon to scapegoat. This means if a corporate or political leader is guilty of wrongdoing, she finds an innocent person to take the blame for her. Of course at this level, whoever takes the fall is usually destroyed and finished in business or politics.

Sometimes the fall guy fully understands what he's getting himself into. In other situations, the sacrifice is forced upon him. If he could do something about it he would, but they know he doesn't have the resources to fight these corporate or political giants through due process. And even if he tried to fight back, they would destroy him through "terrorism by litigation."

Collateral Damage!— All of It.

Why Jesus Didn't Stop Judas From Betraying Him—

Jesus knew what His true purpose for being made flesh and dwelling among men was. He knew had to give His life on the cross. Had Jesus not gone to the cross, all the prophecies would be lies... and all the prophets would be liars. *"Do you think that I cannot appeal to My Father, and He will at once put at My disposal more than twelve legions of angels? How then will the Scriptures be fulfilled, which say that it must happen this way?"* Matthew 26:53-54

Had someone not betrayed Jesus, the crucifixion might not have happened. Judas Iscariot was that someone. He entered into a deal with the religious leaders to capture and arrest Jesus. Thirty (30) pieces of silver was the price for which Judas Iscariot betrayed Jesus.

> *"Then one of the twelve, named Judas Iscariot, went to the chief priests and said, 'What are you willing to give me to betray Him to you?' And they weighed out thirty pieces of silver to him."*
>
> Matthew 26:14-15

There would be no wonderful plan of salvation and redemption had Jesus not gone to the cross to be crucified. And, there would be no gift of the Holy Ghost as Jesus promised in the 14th Chapter of St. John.

> *"But the Comforter, which is the Holy Ghost, whom the Father will send in my name, he shall teach you all things, and bring all things to your remembrance, whatsoever I have said unto you."*
>
> John 14:26 (KJV)

After Judas' betrayal, when the soldiers came to apprehend Him, Peter drew his sword to fight them off. Jesus told Peter to put his sword away. His knew his own death was necessary.

As with all of us, Judas was granted free-will to choose right from wrong. But of course, God saw the vile in Judas before Judas was even born. Someone had to betray Him. Judas was that someone. Here's what Jesus said about Judas:

> "For the Son of Man must die, as the Scriptures declared long ago. But how terrible it will be for the one who betrays him. It would be far better for that man if he had never been born!"
>
> Matthew 26:24 (NLT)

**In God's master plan of redemption—
Judas Iscariot was indeed... Collateral Damage!**

"While most nations on the planet were busy worrying about a nuclear missile strike... the world got hit by something far worse —A Virus!"

Frank Jackson

Chapter Five

MAKING SENSE OF PANDEMIC VIRUSES

"The Characteristics Of Viruses"

There's no denying it. The novel coronavirus has turned the world upside down. Sports, entertainment, school, extra-curricula and work— *All Canceled!* Much of the world has been frightened into a tail-spin. Planet Earth reached a near standstill.

What I am feeling while writing this book must be what the late, great writer, Orson Wells must have felt when he set out to write the novel "1984." No, greatness isn't what I am referring to. I'm sure anyone could have written my book. It didn't necessarily have to be me. But, what I'm talking about is the hesitation you feel when writing significantly about the future.

COVID-19 AND THE CHURCH
by Frank and Annese Jackson

Orson Wells (who was born George Orwells) a Kenosha, Wisconsin (USA) native who was born on May 6, 1915 wrote the 1949 novel "1984" in the aftermath of World War II, during tense and shifting political climates. The novel depicts a dystopian future in which the citizens of Oceania live in misery, under constant surveillance.

The problem with writing about the future is you can be easily proven wrong. Orson Wells was deemed brilliant for his fictional depiction of a futuristic society. But, when the year 1984 actually arrived, he could have also been declared an erroneous fool.

As the year of 1984 approached, I'm sure Orson Wells was relieved to be able to see and confirm that his fictitious prediction was just that... fiction! Oddly, he lived just (barely) long enough to see the year of 1984 come and go. Orson Wells died on October 10, 1985 In Los Angeles, California (USA).

Deadliest 21St Century Plague To Hit The U.S.—

When the new novel coronavirus disease spread rapidly around throughout world, it was officially declared a pandemic by the World Health Organization (WHO) on March 11, 2020. By then, millions of people had already been infected and the death toll had risen to well over 171,000 souls. I suspect that things will never go back to what we call normal. The world as we know it, may be over.

Unmistakably, the new modern times COVID pales in comparison to other past plagues that have caused much devastation throughout the world. However, for those in the United States and many other countries, the coronavirus might be their deadliest nightmare of the

21st Century. It would be great if this pandemic turned out to be just as imaginary as the novel "1984." But that will never be.

By the time this book has reached your hands, the number of confirmed cases worldwide, as well as the number of deaths, may have already grown beyond human imagination. I hope I'm wrong.

Honestly, my hope and prayer are by the time this book hits Amazon, Barnes & Noble or the store shelves, a cure will have been discovered to cause my statements here to be as invalid and unfounded as Orson Wells' predictions for 1984. In this particular case, I would rather be absolutely wrong than to be absolutely right.

At this time I would like to explain viruses in general. But before we continue, I should qualify my position. I realize that my job (here) isn't to give you a crash course on viruses. However, I firmly believe when anything has the capacity to destroy an earthly civilization, we should know something about it.

***Important Note:**

The remainder of this chapter gives in-depth information on the nature of viruses in general. If you have no desire to understand viruses and how they are structured... no problem. That's okay.

Simply skip the rest of this chapter, and proceed directly to Chapter Six (6). This will not affect your outcome with this book. You'll be just fine. However, if you are interested in knowing how viruses work, please continue with this chapter.

Understanding Viruses

Now, for those of you who are interested in acquiring a better understanding concerning one of the worse enemies of your lifetime, thank you for staying with us through this chapter. Educating yourself about current disease outbreaks can help you understand what precautions you should take in order to keep you and your family safe and healthy.

This will be brief. You may need to read slow, and you may also need to read these words several times in order to grasp them.

Since most people confuse viruses with bacteria, and bacteria with viruses... let's start out by pinpointing what a virus really is. In a 2016 Live Science published report, Aparna Vidyasagar tells us, "Viruses are microscopic parasites, generally much smaller than bacteria. They lack the capacity to thrive and reproduce outside of a host body." Now, while a virus may not be able to cause devastation outside of a person or animal, they are able to latch onto host cells and enter them.

According to David Baltimore in a Michigan State University lecture, "a virus is made up of a core of genetic material, either DNA or RNA, surrounded by a protective coat called a capsid which is made up of protein. Sometimes the capsid is surrounded by an additional spikey coat called the envelope. Viruses are capable of latching onto host cells and getting inside them."

In general, viruses are widely known for being the driving force behind the spread of infectious diseases. This has a lot to do with previous deadly outbreaks that resulted in widespread disease and death.

CHAPTER 5　　MAKING SENSE OF PANDEMIC VIRUSES

This Isn't America's First Bout With An Outbreak—

Outbreaks in America date as far back as the 17th-Century, when Smallpox came to North America killing over 70 percent of the Native American population. Entire Native American tribes were destroyed, between 1633 and 1634.

Yellow fever, cholera, scarlet fever, typhoid fever, influenza virus (the Spanish flu), diphtheria, polio, measles, pertussis (known as whooping cough), and AIDS (the final stage of HIV) have all struck North America, collectively killing millions.

In 2009 to 2010, some of our younger Americans may have been too young to understand what was taking place. That was when the Swine flu pandemic killed over 200,000 people, and the United States was hit hard.

However, America's recent Coronavirus outbreaks could never measure up to the 2014 Ebola epidemic in West Africa killing 11,000,300 people. Or the more than two million lives that were taken by the Asian Flu from 1956 to 1958. And, especially not to HIV/AIDS with 25 to 35 million dead (and counting) from 1981 to the present.

Hands down though, the Spanish Flu has been the most lethal in the 20th and 21st centuries... killing between 40 and 50 million people in just under two years, from 1918 to 1919. As with the case of the modern-day COVID, Spanish flu was also introduced into the air through coughing.

The coronavirus virus is in droplets that are released into the air when an infected person coughs, sneezes or exhales. There were those who worked hard at avoiding anyone who was sneezing or coughing, but still contracted the coronavirus.

That confused a lot of people, until new information was released. We now know that a person doesn't have to cough or sneeze on you for you to contract the coronavirus. You can get it by just passing through an area where an infected person is talking, or simply breathing.

As we stated earlier, the new novel coronavirus is definitely not the worse virus to wreak havoc upon the world, but it is clearly a new experience for the majority of 21st-Century Americans. This may account for why so many U.S. citizens made light of the coronavirus... including America's own president, Donald J. Trump.

It may also explain why so many Americans were careless, to the point of disregard for executive orders to shelter-in-place or stay home in quarantine. Sadly, too many Americans failed to respect the COVID for the killer that it has proven itself to be, even as the deaths toll continued to soar beyond belief.

Although the pandemic was becoming more and more deadly, world leaders continued to downplay the severity of the coronavirus.

Misleading and perhaps even confusing and mixed messages from our top leaders around the globe, may have caused a late start for the countries that these leaders represented. This resulted in an enormous death toll.

Because world leaders in China, Italy, Spain, Iran, Brazil, and the United States of America, to name a few, did not take the coronavirus seriously at the start, they may have put their countries at greater risk for infection.

Furthermore, their refusal to ban travel, and to enforce social-distancing may have greatly contributed to the rapid spread of the virus.

The Characteristics Of Viruses—

Like all living things, viruses have specific characteristics that aid professionals by making them more identifiable.

The person or animal infected with the virus is called the host. The particulars of reproduction and virus infection often differ drastically from one host to another, based on the host type.

What we know is all viruses have in common, six (6) basic steps in their reproduction cycles. These six basic steps are: 1) attachment; 2) penetration; 3) uncoating; 4) reproduction; 5) assemblage; 6)release.

1. *First, the virus must attach itself to the host cell.*
2. *Next, penetration of either the contents of the capsid only, or of the whole virus happens.*
3. *In the case of full capsid entry, uncoating of the genetic material takes place to make it accessible by the cell's reproduction system.*
4. *Genetic material reproduction and capsid and tail proteins are next.*
5. *Individual virus particles are assembled, after the reproduction of the needed parts is completed.*
6. *Finally, release takes place, but usually in a rather pernicious way, exploding or erupting while killing the host cell.*

Sure, we've all heard about the novel coronavirus pandemic, but how many people understand what a pandemic really is... aside from being a sickness that causes sickness to millions, and in thousands of cases... death?

For many people, words like epidemic, pandemic, epicenter and hotspot can cause much alarm. Perhaps you're wondering what all of these words mean. Well, let me help you with that right now.

Outbreaks, Epidemics, Pandemics And Epicenters—

Throughout history, nothing has killed more human beings worldwide, than infectious disease. The coronavirus shows how vulnerable we remain— and how we can avoid similar pandemics in the future.

The new COVID had a lot of people confused about how to rate it. Some disaster laymen didn't know whether to call it an epidemic or pandemic. Others were calling it an outbreak. This section explains the differences between an outbreak, an epidemic and a pandemic.

Understanding An Outbreak?

Whenever authorities first announce the presence of a menacing infectious disease such as the coronavirus, to the general population, it is commonly introduced as an outbreak. This means that within a particular geographical region there has been a rapid increase in cases. At this point, any sort of disease outbreak in a localized area could very well be called an epidemic as well.

When reporting on the sudden spreading of an infectious disease over a region, news journalists commonly describe the dilemma as an outbreak. But, when government officials, medical spokespersons and scientific authorities speak, they use more precise terminology.

They must exercise professional precautions, so as to not to send a message to the general public that could cause them to think that a particular localized infectious disease outbreak is a pandemic. To do so could create unnecessary mass panic.

Understanding An Epidemic?

To be classified as an epidemic, the disease generally affects many individuals simultaneously. Additionally, it spreads from person to person in a locality where this particular disease is not predominantly established.

The World Health Organization (WHO) classifies an outbreak as an epidemic when the spread reaches the level where a region or community is affected. For example, WHO will refer to a flu outbreak across the city of Detroit as a citywide flu epidemic.

While the word epidemic is a noun, in this case it could also be an adjective in other cases. So, when we hear WHO refer to a disease an "epidemic disease," they are using the word epidemic as an adjective to describe the seriousness of the outbreak. The same applies to the word pandemic.

Understanding A Pandemic?

One of the easiest ways to describe a pandemic might be to look at it as an epidemic that has grown far beyond a localized community. In simple terms, the infectious disease has now spread over a country, a continent or the entire world.

In the interest of greater clarity, the World Health Organization defines a pandemic as "a worldwide spread of a new disease." On March 11, 2020, WHO officially announced to the world that the Coronavirus outbreak has spread around the world and is now officially upgraded to a pandemic.

Explaining An Epicenter?

An epicenter may also be called a hotspot or a hot zone. In the case of a pandemic, the epicenter is essentially, the focal point of the pandemic. When any region, city, state or country is specifically named by WHO as the epicenter of a pandemic disease, that is critical information. What WHO means is, "disproportionately a greater number of confirmed (or increasing) cases are coming from that particular zone, than from any other place in the world."

Local And State Officials Had To Think Outside The Box—

The coronavirus pandemic led to many unanticipated problems. One such problem was, how to handle and treat the unprecedented number of people showing up at hospital emergency centers with coronavirus symptoms. Another mind draining problem was what to do with massive numbers of human bodies that were collecting across the U.S. and around the world.

In the United States, state and local officials had to think outside of the box to come up with an answer to that question. These problems had to be solved across the nation without over stressing or offending loved ones.

Illinois's Response To Elevated New Patients Count—

In Illinois, Governor JB Pritzker and Mayor Lori Lightfoot took matters to a whole new level. They brought in the National Guard and Army Corps of Engineers to convert the world-famous McCormick Place Exposition Center into an emergency treatment center for an expected three-thousand (3,000) new coronavirus patients. Fortunately, new patient numbers in Chicago began to decline before all three-thousand mock hospital rooms were completed.

Dealing With Record Numbers Of Human Remains—

Many funeral homes were immediately overloaded to the point of having to process bodies without embalming them. And, Cook County Board President Toni Preckwinkle rose to the challenge by converting a 66,000 square-foot refrigerated warehouse into a morgue. Preckwinkle's make-shift could temporarily store as many as two-thousand (2,000) human remains for several months.

Mass Graves—

But, as bad as things may have been in Chicago, I believe New York might have been hit the hardest of all U.S. cities. In many parts of the world, various countries and localities have had to become creative in their dealings with the excessive amounts of bodies, including cremation and mass graves.

This all led to the widespread usage of refrigerated trucks, refrigerated storage containers, refrigerated buildings, refrigerated anything! In New York, they had to use refrigerated trucks, mass graves and other unorthodox methods and resources to help solve their human remains problem.

No nation of civilized people can possibly get used to (or acclimated to) the sorrow, misery and grief left behind by virus outbreaks. And, it doesn't matter whether they reach epidemic or pandemic proportions, the aftermath is absolute devastation.

So…"What Is A Virus?"

A virus is one of the ugliest and deadliest killers imaginable. Deadlier and more calculating than any enemy missile attack. Their ability to inflict carnage defies all human imagination. No man-made weapon has the capacity to leave behind the horror that a pandemic level virus can. And, no country has the power, knowledge, need or desire to strike every known country on earth at the same time… including themselves.

On the other hand, viruses do have the power and to strike, maim and kill globally… with no regard for gender, age, religious creed, national origin or status in life. Viruses will (and have) attack and afflict anyone from the homeless to heads of state.

Viruses don't care if you are a muscular bodybuilder, a senile old-woman, a crippled old man suffering from Alzheimer's, a disabled child or a newborn baby. Anyone could be a target.

"While most nations on the planet were busy worrying about a nuclear missile strike... the world got hit by something far worse —A Virus!"

"Throughout history, nothing has killed more human beings worldwide, than infectious diseases. the COVID shows how vulnerable we still are!"

Chapter Six

WHY GOD ALLOWS PANDEMIC DISEASES

*"Why Doesn't God Stop
So Many People From Dying?"*

A number of outbreaks of pandemic diseases, such as Ebola, Swine Flu, and a host of several lethal Influenzas, and the novel coronavirus, have concerned people around the world asking "why God allows pandemic level illnesses and widespread death."

With millions of people having been afflicted and hundreds of thousands of deaths throughout the world, some blame God for causing the coronavirus pandemic. Hundreds of millions of people are numbed by the sobering thought that the God of divine love could cause such global upheaval. Others are asking whether the more recent epidemics and pandemics are New Testament signs of the world as we know it.

In the Old Testament, God didn't just allow killer plagues and diseases, He sent them.

> *"For I will at this time send all my plagues upon thine heart, and upon thy servants, and upon thy people; that thou mayest know that there is none like me in all the earth.*
>
> *For now I will stretch out my hand, that I may smite thee and thy people with pestilence; and thou shalt be cut off from the earth.*
>
> *And in very deed for this cause have I raised thee up, for to shew in thee my power; and that my name may be declared throughout all the earth."*
>
> Exodus 9:14-16 (KJV)

"God visited deadly plagues upon Egypt to force Pharaoh's hands in releasing the Israelites from bondage and captivity. He did this while protecting His own people from being harmed by the plagues."

> *"The blood will be a sign for you on the houses where you are, so that when I see the blood I will pass over you, and this plague will not fall on you to destroy you when I attack the land of Egypt."*
>
> Exodus 12:13 (NET)

In the Old Testament, God clearly demonstrated His sovereign control over sickness and diseases. However, His promise of protection and blessings were conditional.

> *"And said, If thou wilt diligently hearken to the voice of the Lord thy God, and wilt do that which is right in his sight, and wilt give ear to his commandments, and*

> keep all his statutes, I will put none of these diseases upon thee, which I have brought upon the Egyptians: for I am the Lord that healeth thee."
> Exodus 15:26 (KJV)

People want to know if a loving God is capable of mass death and devastation. In the book of Leviticus, He warned His people of the consequences they would face if they disobeyed Him.

> "And if ye walk contrary unto me, and will not hearken unto me; I will bring seven times more plagues upon you according to your sins."
> Leviticus 26:21 (KJV)

In two (2) separate incidents, God killed 14,700 people, then 24,000 more, all for disobedience.

> "Now they that died in the plague were fourteen thousand and seven hundred" Numbers 16:49 (KJV)

> "And those that died in the plague were twenty and four thousand." Numbers 25:9 (KJV)

Just as God promises blessings those who obey and keep His commandments, He also promises disaster to those who rebelliously refuse to.

I realize it's hard to wrap your mind around a merciful God full of love, sending so much mayhem upon His people. But in the Bible, God's punishment usually led to repentance and restoration.

God told Solomon:

> "If I shut up heaven that there be no rain, or if I command the locusts to devour the land, or if I send pestilence among my people;

> "If my people, which are called by my name, shall

humble themselves, and pray, and seek my face, and turn from their wicked ways; then will I hear from heaven, and will forgive their sin, and will heal their land." 2 Chronicles 7:13-14

In the Old Testament, God chose to use plagues and diseases to demonstrate His power. But, in the New Testament Jesus went about healing illnesses and diseases in displaying God's power and to draw people to the Lord.

"And Jesus went about all the cities and villages, teaching in their synagogues, and preaching the gospel of the kingdom, and healing every sickness and every disease among the people."

Matthew 9:35 (KJV)

"For he had healed many; insomuch that they pressed upon him for to touch him, as many as had plagues." Mark 3:10 (KJV)

"And when he had called unto him his twelve disciples, he gave them power against unclean spirits, to cast them out, and to heal all manner of sickness and all manner of disease."

Matthew 10:1 (KJV)

This display of healing miracles proved to be solid evidence to many that Jesus was indeed, the Son of God. Throughout the New Testament, we read where Jesus also passed this same healing power on to His disciples.

"Then he called his twelve disciples together, and gave them power and authority over all devils, and to cure diseases." Luke 9:1 (KJV)

We know that God allows pestilences and pandemics today, because of the fallen world in which we live.

Aside from divine knowledge or visitation, it would be impossible to know for sure whether or not a particular outbreak has a deep spiritual purpose behind it. What we do know for certain is God in control of everything. Nothing can happen on planet earth without God's own permission. He will always have the final say.

The Coronavirus May Be Just...
"A Preview of Coming Attractions"

What Next?... Stacked Pandemics! While this book is being written, global conditions are rapidly changing around us. It's hard to keep up with everything that's going on. As we write, there is now concern about the threat of a new strain of flu that comes at a time when the world is already broken down from the coronavirus.

Modern pandemics are frightening at the very least, but they are only a sneak preview of what is to come. In the New Testament, Jesus predicted that there would be plagues to usher in the end times.

> *"And great earthquakes shall be in divers places, and famines, and pestilences; and fearful sights and great signs shall there be from heaven."*
>
> Luke 21:11 (KJV)

The book Revelation tells us of the two (2) witnesses who will have the power to attack our whole planet with any plague of their choosing, whenever and as often as they please.

> *"These have the power to shut up the sky, so that rain will not fall during the days of their prophesying; and they have power over the waters to turn them into blood, and to strike the earth with every plague, as often as they desire."*
>
> Revelation 11:6 (NASB)

Whenever there is a pandemic, people die; a lot of people die. It would be hard for us to accurately identify modern pandemics as end-time shreds of evidence. Mainly, because none of us know for sure when Jesus will return. It isn't wise to rush to connect any pandemic to God's definite judgment of sin on earth. It could just be one of the things that happen when we live in a fallen world.

So, it behooves us to be careful about calling any particular pandemic, the end-time Judgment of God. I'm not saying you're not right. What I am saying is you just don't know for certain.

However, the COVID and any other epidemics or pandemics that this world has witnessed are like a hangnail compared to what is to come.

The 16th chapter of Revelation gives a terrifying report of the dread that seven (7) angels on a mission, will release upon the earth. We've never done this before, but this message is so alarming that we decided to include the entire 16th chapter of Revelation here:

"Then I heard a loud voice from the temple declaring to the seven angels: "Go and pour out on the earth the seven bowls containing God's wrath." So the first angel went and poured out his bowl on the earth. Then ugly and painful sores appeared on the people who had the mark of the beast and who worshiped his image.

Next, the second angel poured out his bowl on the sea and it turned into blood, like that of a corpse, and every living creature that was in the sea died.

Then the third angel poured out his bowl on the rivers and the springs of water, and they turned into blood. Now I heard the angel of the waters saying:

'You are just—the one who is and who was, the Holy One—because you have passed these judgments, because they poured out the blood of your saints and prophets, so you have given them blood to drink. They got what they deserved!'

Then I heard the altar reply, 'Yes, Lord God, the All-Powerful, your judgments are true and just!'

Then the fourth angel poured out his bowl on the sun, and it was permitted to scorch people with fire. Thus people were scorched by the terrible heat, yet they blasphemed the name of God, who has ruling authority over these plagues, and they would not repent and give him glory.

Then the fifth angel poured out his bowl on the throne of the beast so that darkness covered his kingdom, and people began to bite their tongues because of their pain. They blasphemed the God of heaven because of their sufferings and because of their sores, but nevertheless they still refused to repent of their deeds.

Then the sixth angel poured out his bowl on the great river Euphrates and dried up its water to prepare the way for the kings from the east. Then I saw three unclean spirits that looked like frogs coming out of the mouth of the dragon, out of the mouth of the beast, and out of the mouth of the false prophet. For they are the spirits of the demons performing signs who go out to the kings of the earth to bring them together for the battle that will take place on the great day of God, the All-Powerful.

(Look! I will come like a thief! Blessed is the one who stays alert and does not lose his clothes so that he will not have to walk around naked and his shameful condition be seen.)

> *Now the spirits gathered the kings and their armies to the place that is called Armageddon in Hebrew.*
>
> *Finally the seventh angel poured out his bowl into the air and a loud voice came out of the temple from the throne, saying: 'It is done!'*
>
> *Then there were flashes of lightning, roaring, and crashes of thunder, and there was a tremendous earthquake—an earthquake unequaled since humanity has been on the earth, so tremendous was that earthquake. The great city was split into three parts and the cities of the nations collapsed.*
>
> *So Babylon the great was remembered before God, and was given the cup filled with the wine made of God's furious wrath. Every island fled away and no mountains could be found. And gigantic hailstones, weighing about a 100 pounds each, fell from heaven on people, but they blasphemed God because of the plague of hail, since it was so horrendous."*
>
> Revelation 16:1-21 (NET)

We all know, that there is no such thing as a good pandemic. All pandemics are bad... real bad! But, hell is worse... "Much Worse!"

Disasters should serve as a reminder to us of how fragile our existence here on earth really is. The book of James tells us that... our time here is for only a brief moment. As a direct result of the coronavirus, thousands of people died within a few days. This is a testimony that any of us can be gone in a moment.

> *"Yet you do not know what your life will be like tomorrow. You are just a vapor that appears for a little while and then vanishes away."*
>
> James 4:14 (NASB)

We are nothing more than a vapor, or a mist that appears for a moment and then disappears. So, whatever a mist has to accomplish... must be done before it vanishes. And, whatever, you have to do... must be done before your life is over. This may involve fulfilling your commitments to the Lord. Or for you it may mean, getting right with God.

Because of the blood that Jesus shed for our sins, believers have the blessed assurance of salvation and the hope of eternal life with Jesus Christ.

"But he was wounded for our transgressions, he was bruised for our iniquities: the chastisement of our peace was upon him; and with his stripes we are healed."

Isaiah 53:5 (KJV)

"For he hath made him to be sin for us, who knew no sin; that we might be made the righteousness of God in him."

2 Corinthians 5:21

"Do not dread the disease that stalks in darkness... though ten thousand are dying around you, these evils will not touch you!"   Psalm 91:5-7

Chapter Seven

3-REASONS WHY THE QUARANTINE IS BIBLICAL

"We're Just Asking You To Shut Down Your Church Building... Not the Church!"

When we talk about the consequential (collateral) damage of the coronavirus, we immediately think of essential workers like... doctors, nurses, police officers, firefighters ambulance workers and other first Responders. And, we must not forget transportation workers, daycare workers and other essential workers, like my daughter who happens to be a scientist.

During the COVID's most frightening time, several pastors said, they would not be closing their church, or complying with the executive "shelter-at-home" order.

Their reasoning was, because they believed the church was just as essential as healthcare professionals, law enforcement officers and first responders.

They sure got an awful lot of "Amens" and high fives for that one. The members loved it. Perhaps, these pastors and their members didn't realize they could continue church without putting the people they serve, at risk for the coronavirus. They weren't ordered to shut down the church... just the buildings.

But, if that's how these preachers really feel, that's okay. However, they should be aware that the essential workers in every field just named, understand that they are risking their lives to accomplish their tasks.

They believe so much in what they're doing, that they're willing to "put their lives" on the line. Many of these brave men and women have died... and no one is surprised. It's all part of being essential. So, why is the church so surprised when "essential" workers of the cloth die from the virus, the same as all the others?

Preachers Refuse To Believe Their Own Preaching—

It would be wonderful if they really believed what they are saying. Keep in mind the coronavirus is a new experience for the modern church. We've been preaching about "end-time" famines and plagues for centuries. But when they finally strike, preachers refuse to believe their own preaching.

I honestly don't think most of these "essential" pastors understood (or understand, even now) God's hand in this lethal COVID. Pastors and Bishops are accustomed to being in control of things. They get uncomfortable when they're not personally dictating their church's every movement.

The book of James should serve as a reminder to us that we are not in control... God is:

> *"Now listen, you who say... 'Today or tomorrow we will go to this or that city, spend a year there, carry on business and make money.'*
>
> *Why, you do not even know what will happen tomorrow. What is your life? You are a mist that appears for a little while and then vanishes. Instead, you ought to say, If it is the Lord's will, we will live and do this or that."*
>
> James 4:13-15

Too many preachers have been unaccountable for so long, to the point where they actually believed they were beyond the reach of the coronavirus. To them, death by a pandemic virus is something that happens at other churches, and to other people. Not to them.

Now, here's where the water gets muddied. They think their members may be okay, but they're not sure. But, they are willing to gamble the lives of their members. If no one dies from the virus, the pastor comes out of it looking like a god (small "g"). If a member does die...? Well, my guess is they figured they would cross that bridge when they got to it.

But the bottom line is this— they were aware that there is a chance that things may not go as planned. Non-compliance to the quarantine order means members of the church may die.

These preachers watched the very graphic news reporting of the virus, just like everyone else. An astounding number of church leaders and church members started dying early on in the pandemic. In fact, one global denomination lost dozens of their bishops, and perhaps hundreds of their congregates to the coronavirus, within just a few short weeks.

Although the stakes are high, many leaders are still willing to risk the lives of non-family members. Mainly, because their concern for preserving the revenue to continue fueling their family businesses, is greater than their concern for the safety of the members of their churches.

Three (3) Bible Points Concerning Quarantines—

Now, I realize that there have been men and women of God who sincerely believe in their hearts that to carry on their assembled worship services, is what God wants. But, they are sincerely wrong. We know this because the Bible speaks of quarantines.

This isn't biblical leadership— Real people are dying. Church people are dying. Church leaders are dying! *"What are you thinking???"* God gives us concise instructions on how to deal with calamities and pandemics.

I don't even understand the churches that had skeleton crews to assemble at the church, to present praise worship, while the parishioners view from the safety of their homes. Now you're putting your skeleton crew at risk!

1. Go Into Your Home And Close The Door—

These religious leaders had even tried to dictate the movement and actions of the **coronavirus**. They've been telling their members to disregard the official shelter-at-home order, and to trust God to protect them. And, I get that, but the Bible tells us that we have a role or duty concerning God's protection during a divinely orchestrated or permitted march of death.

The book of Isaiah teaches us that just because we believe in God and work in the church, doesn't automatically exempt us from pain or suffering. Being a believer or doing the right things does not mean you will be spared from earthly harm, sickness, or suffering. We live in a fallen, sinful world that is filled with sickness and suffering. And, we can at any time find ourselves in harm's way.

There are many Bible verses that speak of quarantine. Some verses talk about quarantine as a method for cleansing the body from affliction. Other passages talk about quarantine as a protective hedge to the people of God when they live in obedience to Him.

One such scripture has been bouncing around ever since the coronavirus hit the United States. After hearing about or reading Isaiah 26:20, for the first time most churchgoers learn that quarantines are actually biblical.

> *"Go home, my people, and lock your doors! Hide yourselves for a little while until the Lord's anger has passed."* Isaiah 26:20 (NLT)

Many Bible scholars are quick to point out that this is (more likely than not) words to a song, rather than a word from the lord. The truth is, even if it is song lyrics it doesn't matter. It doesn't take away from the integrity of these words nor their validity as a directive from the Lord.

The book of Psalms is largely about songs, but rarely does anyone say, *"because these are songs their words are irrelevant."* True believers live and die by the words of the psalmists.

The book of Psalms was considered to be the hymnbook of the Old Testament Israelites. Most people in the church believe all of the psalms were written by King David of Israel. But, David is credited with having written only seventy-three (73) psalms of the one hundred and fifty (150) psalms.

Other contributors of the very poetic book of Psalms were Asaph (and family), The sons of Korah, Heman, Solomon, Moses, Ethan the Ezrahite, and other anonymous psalmists. Even though there were many writers of Psalms, hardly any true believer would take the words of the psalmists as merely entertaining songs.

It isn't unusual for people to be highly blessed by the comforting lyrics of the 27th Psalm:

"The Lord is my light and my salvation; whom shall I fear? The Lord is the strength of my life; of whom shall I be afraid?"

When the wicked, even mine enemies and my foes, came upon me to eat up my flesh, they stumbled and fell.

Though an host should encamp against me, my heart shall not fear: though war should rise against me, in this will I be confident.

One thing have I desired of the Lord, that will I seek after; that I may dwell in the house of the Lord all the days of my life, to behold the beauty of the Lord, and to enquire in his temple."

Psalm 27:1-4

And, how many times have we found comfort assurance and strength in the 23rd psalms:

> "The Lord is my shepherd... I shall not want."
>
> Psalm 23:1

My point is, if Isaiah 26:20-21 is part of the words to a song—*So What!* If we throw out the 26th chapter of Isaiah as just another song, then we need to throw out the 23rd psalm with it.

Furthermore, throughout the ages, oppressed people have used music as a means of secretly communicating with one another. Messages and stories were hidden in the lyrics and the rhythm and beats of the music. This enabled them to communicate secretly without their oppressors knowing that they were actually talking to each other.

Additionally, there have been many instances where God has communicated with His children, through music. So, when God's warning says— *"Go home, my people, and lock your doors! Hide yourselves for a little while until the Lord's anger has passed,"* believe Him... even if the warning comes by way of a song.

2. Trust The Lord—

God has promised to protect those of us who place our faith and trust in Him. His covering can protect us from the fiery darts of the wicked. In the 91st psalm, the psalmist says:

> *"You need not fear the terrors of the night, the arrow that flies by day, the plague that stalks in the darkness, or the disease that ravages at noon. Though a thousand may fall beside you, and a multitude on your right side, it will not reach you."* Psalm 91:5-7

But, we must understand that God usually requires that we do something to put our faith into action. Before He raised His dear friend Lazarus from the dead, He had the people to roll the stone away from the opening of the tomb. Before He changed water into wine, He had them to fill the pots to the brim with water.

Now, you would think that if He could raise the dead or change water to wine He could roll the stone away himself, or make wine flow from the empty pots. Of course He could have. That was the easy part. But, He wants us to put forth the effort to set faith into motion. Then, when we do what we can do, He does what we can't do. If we roll away the stone, He'll raise the dead. If we obey His command, He'll perform the miracle.

This was their way of demonstrating faith in His mighty power to perform miracles. So, if we truly believe His promise to protect us from the novel coronavirus, or any other virus, He will. But, we must obey His directions in order for that to happen. The bible says:

> *"For just as the body without the spirit is dead, so also faith without works is dead."* James 2:26 (KJ21)

Our part is simple. All we have to do is quarantine ourselves. He'll do the rest.

3. Respect Our Government Officials—

Next, we must be obedient to God when it comes to respecting the guidance and the executive directives of our government leaders. During the new COVID pandemic, world leaders ordered their citizens to quarantine themselves.

When an executive order to shelter at home is issued by our mayor, governor… or our president, unless it violates our biblical convictions, we should take heed.

> "Every person is to be in subjection to the governing authorities. For there is no authority except from God, and those which exist are established by God."
>
> Romans 13:1

What Should We Do In The Midst Of Uncertainty?—

First of all, learn to be thankful in all situations. Trials and tribulations will come our way, but God is always in control.

> "In everything give thanks: for this is the will of God in Christ Jesus concerning you."
>
> 1 Thessalonians 5:18 (KJV)

Of course you should be grateful, but being grateful in the midst of trials does not mean that Christians are to be passionless or numb. Being thankful doesn't mean that believers don't feel emotion or pain.

> "To those who have sorrow in Zion I will give them a crown of beauty instead of ashes. I will give them the oil of joy instead of sorrow,
>
> and a spirit of praise instead of a spirit of no hope. Then they will be called oaks that are right with God, planted by the Lord, that He may be honored."
>
> Isaiah 61:3 (NLV)

Sometimes, praise is necessary when you are hurting and suffering. Just as we must know He is always here for us, we must also know, we are safe in His hands.

Quarantine is a great time to tighten your connection with God. Spend time in prayer and Bible study; even fasting and consecration. Take advantage of the opportunity that God provides for you to bless or encourage someone else.

You can still share the gospel with others from home; share your hardship and share how God is with you every step of the way. Let them know that it's not easy, sometimes we fail to remember God's promises, sometimes we fail to enjoy God's presence—but there's grace, abounding grace, because of the sacrifice Jesus made for us.

His life covers all our misdeeds, our doubts, our caved temptations—through the helper He left us with. Through God the Holy Spirit, we are being sanctified each day for our good and God's glory.

When it comes to quarantining yourself and your family, remember the words of the psalmist:

> *"Do not dread the disease that stalks in darkness, nor the disaster that strikes at midday. Though a thousand fall at your side, though ten thousand are dying around you, these evils will not touch you."*
>
> Psalms 91:6-7 (NLT)

"Many animals are more sanitary than some humans!"

Annese Jackson

Chapter Eight

PUBLIC ENEMY #1— HUMANS!

*"Diseases Travel Throughout
The World By Humans"*

As humans move all around the world... so do lethal and infectious diseases. Humans are by far the single greatest transmitters of infectious diseases.

The coronavirus is credited for giving us a new word; "zoonotic" meaning the viruses are transmitted between animals and people. According to the Center for Disease Control (CDC) *"6 in 10 Infectious Diseases Come from Animals."*

Pigs, bats, rats, bugs and birds are just a few of the animal culprits named by leading authorities on pandemic diseases. In some cases, humans were bitten by an animal or insect. It isn't always easy to avoid bug bites.

What is much easier to avoid, is eating untested, unpreserved, and unrefrigerated animals. So many people eat disease-infected animals. They themselves contract the deadly disease from the contaminated meat and pass it on to another human; who passes it on to someone else; and so on.

As if this isn't bad enough, the real problem begins when these infected people decide to travel. This is where the disease gets introduced to other regions. As more and more of these individuals travel further and further away from their own hotspots, the spread of the disease is categorically unavoidable.

Many Humans Are Less Sanitary Than Animals—

Although more than half of the infectious diseases that affect people are zoonotic, humans are chiefly responsible for carrying and spreading them.

On top of eating bad meats, humans are some of God's most unsanitary creatures. How many times have you seen someone come in off the street and sit right down at the table to eat; without washing their hands?

They may have (unknowingly) been exposed to a virus. They wouldn't know. Did you ever notice how servers in restaurants hold your drinking glass by placing their hands over the top where your mouth is supposed to go?

And, pay attention to how nurses handle your medications in the hospital. They're pushing a cart around with a computer on top of it. Your medicines are in the drawer beneath the computer shelf.

Even if they wash their hands and put on gloves, that cart that they keep touching isn't sanitary. Remember, it's been in every patient room on that floor, and not once cleaned upon leaving each room.

CHAPTER 8 — PUBLIC ENEMY #1— HUMANS!

Even after they (supposedly) clean their hands, they continue to touch everything around them. At the same time they are treating you, they often go in and out of the door, while touching it with those same gloves. Usually, they will not rewash their hands or change gloves, until after they're done with you.

One nurse went so far as to lift the toilet seat with his hand to dump urine, then he walked over to my bedside to redo the line going into my bloodstream. Of course, I stopped him. Just like I have had to stop nurses who want to handle my medications while wearing contaminated gloves. In many cases, they will actually touch the pills. I wish I had a dollar for every time a nurse said to me, "But I'm wearing gloves!" I always reply, "Well, at least you're protected!"

In my bestselling book, "THUG PREACHERS" I discuss how untold numbers of patients die needlessly each year in America's 5000 hospitals.

The number of deaths was so great that I didn't believe it. I thought it was all just a made-up lie to sensationalize hospital caused deaths. Plus, I was sure that if this was taking place in America, the American Medical Association (AMA), our legislators, or someone would certainly step up to do something about it. Or, it would definitely be all over the news. So, I researched this problem for myself. I was blown away by what I discovered.

We realize that medical professionals at all levels, are at the forefront of saving the lives of coronavirus victims. They've been consistently putting their lives on the line for us during the COVID. I don't know if I could do what they have done, and continue to do. Along with all of our first responders, they've been doing for this country what most others wouldn't even consider doing. They are our true American heroes.

So, we're not crazy. We know this is undeniably, the worse possible time to say anything negative about healthcare workers. So, we would like to include here an excerpt from the previously released book, Thug Preachers. This excerpt is not intended to offend anyone. It is printed here for informational purposes only. If you find it hard to believe I understand. I did too... until I researched its validity.

It's important for you to know that This excerpt must be read with a full understanding that the information here is not an implication of all medical and health professionals. The vast majority of our men and women in medicine are personally invested in, and dedicated to the health and well-being of you and your family. And, we thank them for their dedication.

Excerpt from my book, Thug Preachers:

One afternoon, while researching the spread of disease and infections in hospitals, I came across a very interesting article. It was a post by CNN Senior Medical Correspondent, Elizabeth Cohen. According to this article, Dr. Peter Pronovost, director of the Quality and Safety Research Group at Johns Hopkins University, announced, "About 100,000 people die each year from infections we give them in the hospital."

Dr. Pronovost went on to say, "About 65,000 of those deaths are the result of infections from ventilators and catheters." Here's how he breaks it down. There are about 5,000 hospitals in the United States. So, statistically, each hospital in the United States gives these deadly infections to one patient every month.

PBS TV broadcast journalist, Ray Suarez, joins the growing list of town criers who, like Dr. Peter Pronovost, are calling attention to this healthcare atrocity.

CHAPTER 8 — PUBLIC ENEMY #1— HUMANS!

Suarez says, "The numbers are sobering." He continues, *"The federal government estimates that each year about 100,000 people die in the U.S. after acquiring one or more infections during their stays at a hospital."*

Can you even imagine 100,000 preventable deaths actually occurring in America each year? This number is inconceivable to me, but if there is an ounce of accuracy here, this gross negligence ought to be regarded as criminal.

The death toll from the 911 terrorist attack in New York, was roughly around 3,000. That one massive attack shook up our nation and the world. Now, if my calculations are accurate, it would require terrorists repeating 911 about every 11 days to equal the number of the alleged deaths caused by hospital workers in a single year.

Of course, they would have to do the same thing all over again each year to keep up with the reported annual death toll caused by our hospitals. So, who are America's real terrorists? Then again, that's a whole other story.

There have been a number of investigative news reports, all adding up to the same thing. The fourth major cause of deaths among Americans, behind heart disease, cancer and strokes is hospital infections.

Infections resulting from unsanitary hospital conditions and unsanitary hospital personnel take more lives yearly than fires, automobile accidents and drowning combined.

The fact that handwashing saves lives is not exactly "Breaking News." More than 150 years ago, Dr. Ignaz Semmelweis, a greatly accomplished Hungarian born

> doctor working in the Vienna Hospital, proved that his dirty handed medical staff members were responsible for the high death rate of women after childbirth.
>
> When Dr. Semmelweis, insisted that his fellow doctors and medical students wash their hands before delivering babies, the death rate plunged from 13% to 2% among new mothers in just one month.
>
> This proves that the spread of disease in hospitals is by in large, avoidable. The same applies to the spread of disease (spiritually) in our churches.
>
> End of Excerpt

I've seen signs conspicuously posted around hospitals, informing patients, visitors and workers of the dangers of unwashed hands. They tell us that thousands of patients die each year, due to unwashed hands. I've also seen broadcast announcements aired over the hospital's own television channel, delivering the same message.

At a hospital in Illinois several years ago, the sign on a table in a sitting area indicated that 4,400 patients die in hospitals each year, because of unwashed hands. Well, that's clearly a long way from 100,000 yearly deaths in hospitals.

But, remember, there are other reasons as well. Sixty-five (65) percent of these avoidable deaths are the result of contaminated catheters and breathing equipment. Other reasons for unnecessary hospital deaths include negligence, medical malpractice and a host of other things.

These deaths are preventable. Nonetheless, they continue. If the people who we trust our lives to are this careless and negligent, what can we expect from the average person who hasn't been trained in science and medicine?

Even now, with all of our new modern medical advancements and scientific breakthroughs, infectious disease outbreaks continue to occur. Fortunately though, most of the world is unaware it, because the majority of outbreaks don't reach pandemic proportions, as did the coronavirus.

You get no argument from me; I get it. Most often, animals transmit diseases, but humans are (without a doubt) the guilty parties when it comes to spreading them. Animals don't buy plane tickets, take cruises or pack out stadiums. Nor do animals cough and sneeze all over classrooms, supermarkets, buses and the workplace.

"I suppose as long as there are humans, there will always be pestilences, plagues, infectious diseases, contagious viruses— ***and deadly consequences.****"*

"The price of freedom, respect and human rights around the world has never come cheap."

Annese E. Jackson

Chapter Nine

WHEN TWO MAJOR FORCES COLLIDE

"A Pandemic As the Backdrop of A Global Protest"

As if the world didn't already have its hands full while trying to deal with the coronavirus, political uncertainty, impending threats of war, and racial unrest... another officer-involved killing takes place in the United States.

Officer Derek Chauvin, a veteran of nineteen years with the Minneapolis Police Department, along with three other police officers have all been charged with murder following the arrest, which led to the death of George Floyd. Mr. Floyd, a black man, was suspected of passing counterfeit currency at the local Cup Foods Store.

Police were summoned to the location of the alleged crime, where Mr. Floyd was still present and sitting in a car. Clearly, there was no attempt on the part of Mr. Floyd to flee the scene. Floyd was ordered out of the vehicle by officers Kueng and Lane. Floyd was advised that he was under arrest and placed in handcuffs. He was walked across the street to be placed inside an awaiting police cruiser.

Witnesses say they heard Mr. Floyd tell the officers that he was not resisting, but that he was claustrophobic and did not want to be locked inside the back of a police car. Late to arrive on the scene were training officer, Derek Chauvin and his partner, Officer Tou Thao.

Chauvin assumed command of the arrest. Things get a bit sketchy from there. They had already placed Floyd in the car, but a struggle seemed to ensue. Chauvin pulled Mr. Floyd across the backseat from the driver's side to the passenger side, then out of the vehicle. The suspect was yanked out of the cruiser, smashing to the ground with his hands still handcuffed behind his back.

Now, Floyd lay pinned chest down to the pavement by three (3) of the arresting officers. Officer Kueng was on his back, applying pressure to his torso. Lane knelt on, and applied pressure to his legs while Chauvin knelt on and applied extreme pressure to Floyd's neck. Officer Tou Thao stood guard over the officers, keeping the crowd of concerned onlookers at bay.

Multiple witnesses began to film the encounter from different angles. Widely circulated videos of the arrest went viral on the Internet within hours. Across America and around the world Mr. Floyd can be heard sixteen (16) times saying, "I can't breathe."

CHAPTER 9

WHEN TWO MAJOR FORCES COLLIDE

Floyd had to know he was dying, he had seen the Eric Garner video, and videos of other African American men in this same situation. We've all seen those images. He wasn't the first black man to end up in a struggle for survival with police over a "suspected" minor offense, and he won't be the last.

We can hear him pleading and begging... even calling out, "Mama, Mama!" Floyd's cry for mercy, as well as the admonishments to the officers from the gathered crowd to let him breathe, all fell on deaf ears, as the officers continued to apply even more pressure. Floyd cried out, "Please, the knee in my neck, I can't breathe." Then Floyd gasps, "I'm about to die!" To which Officer Chauvin responded, "Relax."

Eventually, the arresting officers called for an ambulance on a non-emergency basis. About a minute later, they escalated the call to emergency status.

Chauvin continued to kneel on Floyd's neck...even after Floyd appeared to be completely unresponsive. When bystanders confronted the officers about Floyd's condition, Chauvin pulled out mace to keep bystanders away, as Officer Thao moved between them and Chauvin.

Bystanders repeatedly yelled that Floyd was no longer responsive, and urged the officers to check his pulse. Allegedly, Kueng checked Floyd's wrist but found no pulse. Sadly, the officers did not attempt to provide first-aid or CPR for Mr. Floyd.

By now, there are hundreds of copies of the videos showing the arrest and death of George Floyd that have gone viral around the world. To watch a non-violent suspect die at the hands of police officers, right in front of your eyes added a very different dynamic to police brutality.

Numerous anti-police brutality protests broke out across the United States, and later around the world. Cities were set ablaze. Police stations were stormed and destroyed. Police cars were burned, and more people died.

Hundreds of Thousands of People Around the World Came Out of Quarantine to Protest

With the Coronavirus as the backdrop, millions of humans came out of quarantine to participate in the global protests. Some wore protective masks, others did not. And, many of the protesters who did wear masks, some of them just had the masks hanging loosely around their faces or necks.

Some practiced social-distancing, while many were right up in one another's faces. There was also much physical contact between protesters. There was also much close interaction between police officers and protesters.

The battle cry around the world was, "This is too important to allow the coronavirus to keep me in quarantine!" People had pledged to themselves and to their families that they would remain quarantined until the COVID threat was over, or at least under control.

But, when an unarmed George Floyd was killed by Minneapolis police officers, even some of the most dedicated to the quarantine, came out to demonstrate, and to showcase their own outrage.

With the initial stages of the protests behind us, some are beginning to ask important questions like, "Did we make a mistake in coming together with so many strangers?" After all, any of them could have been carrying the COVID.

Many have already begun to think about moments during the protests when they didn't make the best choices in the interest of social-distancing.

With the easing of shelter-at-home executive orders, Memorial Day travel and the reopening of businesses, some states were already seeing a rise in confirmed coronavirus cases. There was already a concern about what we can expect next. Then tragically, another horrific police-involved event took place. And suddenly, protests of outrage broke out in every major part of the United States, and in many significant parts of the world.

WHO Supports The Global Movement Against Racism—

The World Health Organization (WHO) took time during its daily press conference to address the critical issue of sudden wave of protests against police violence against American citizens and racial injustice.

On June 8, 2020 WHO Director-General, Tedros Adhanom Ghebreyesus announced WHO's position on racism. The Director-General said, "WHO fully supports equality and the global movement against racism. We reject discrimination of all kinds"

Although WHO's Ghebreyesus, seemed to imply that the protest might have been necessary as a means of sending a message to world leaders. There did seem to be an indication of concern about following safety guidelines.

Hundreds of thousands of people took to the streets around the world, to demonstrate their outrage against four hundred (400) years of systemic racism, oppression and police brutality. And, to demand equal justice for all African Americans, and swift justice for the family of George Floyd.

In spite of well documented and extreme use of force by heavily militarized police units against protesters and journalists, large protest demonstrations also support another (but unseen) deadly threat. Please be reminded that as these demonstrations were taking place, there was still no medically accepted cure for the coronavirus.

The highly lethal novel coronavirus was (and still is, as of this writing) contagiously circulating in all major parts of the world. We now know that the COVID virus is in droplets that are released into the air when an infected person coughs, sneezes, talks or even exhales.

We also now know that these droplets can remain in the air for up to four (4) hours or more. So, someone can get sick by just passing through an area where an infected person was talking, or simply breathing hours ago.

People Left Their Quarantine To Protest—

Demonstrations against human rights violations and social injustices are a necessary evil of our society in our world: not just America. But we must weigh the risks to our general population. With thousands of protesters shouting, chanting, coughing and sneezing next to one another amid a pandemic, they are always certain to set off a new wave of disease and devastation. We must also consider that tens of thousands of arrested protesters were placed in jails where the coronavirus was already a problem.

There was concern among world health experts that the close contact between thousands of marchers might lead to a spike, when confirmed the COVID cases began to soar. Especially, when 136,000 cases were reported on the first Sunday of the demonstrations in the United States.

The World Health Organization says, that a key ingredient for transmission (close contact) of the coronavirus exists at many protest rallies. Images of large numbers of people standing next to one another, with only some of them wearing masks, is cause for concern, particularly in cities showing higher infection rates.

Public outrage and the coronavirus are two (2) major forces. Health experts are concerned that these two major forces may be on a deadly collision course. Charles Branas, chair of the epidemiology department at Columbia University's Mailman School of Public Health says, "We're really dealing with a syndemic right now, or the compounding effect of multiple, distinct health catastrophes."

Branas goes on to say, "The epidemic of racial injustice has come to a boil alongside an epidemic of the COVID, and they're acting together to really maximize the problem in the US."

Ghebreyesus of WHO, encouraged protesters to listen to and follow the guidance of local health officials. And, to take precautions to protect themselves from the novel coronavirus.

Ghebreyesus went on to say, "We encourage all those protesting around the world to do so safely." He continued, "Clean your hands, cover your cough and wear a mask if you attend a protest." Ghebreyesus also advised protesters to social-distance themselves. He also advised people to stay home if they are sick.

At a WHO press conference, Michael Ryan, director of WHO's health emergencies program said, "The riskiest situation to be in, is to be in close proximity to a case, particularly a symptomatic case, of the COVID." Ryan said, "Healthy people protesting next to one another may not meet the definition of coming in contact with the disease.

According to Director Mike Ryan, researchers now know that the COVID can be spread by people who show no symptoms of it. In fact, it was reported that George Floyd's remains tested positive for the coronavirus during his autopsy.

In the interest of abundance of caution, individuals are advised to either "quarantine or get tested after attending a mass gathering," Ryan said. Nationally, Local officials expressed similar concerns about the connection between the protests and the pandemic.

Bill Miller, an epidemiologist and physician at Ohio State University said, "Testing everyone that participated in demonstrations would be useful in communities where many new cases are being reported every day. These new cases indicate that transmission is occurring at a high rate in the communities."

Miller said an alternative to testing everyone would be to retrace your contact interactions. "With new cases, the tracers could ask about demonstration participation, including days and times," Miller said. Then, if cases are linked to a demonstration, a call could go out to get everyone who participated in that event to be tested."

Apparently, the outdoors may reduce the risk of COVID exposure. The two (2) reasons given are, the virus cannot exist long in sunlight. And, secondly, the outdoors provides better air circulation for warding off the coronavirus. But, there is no real guarantee that being outdoors will protect an individual against any infectious disease.

Freedom Comes At A Price—

The price of freedom, respect and human rights around the world has never come cheap. It has always come at a high price. Often the price has been ultimate.

CHAPTER 9 — WHEN TWO MAJOR FORCES COLLIDE

Many of those who have gone before us, shed their own blood and voluntarily gave up their lives for our freedoms.

In the gospel of St, Mark, we read of a blind man who Jesus laid hands on to restore his sight. This man was previously sighted, but for some reason unknown, he lost his sight. We know this, because the Bible says his sight was restored.

When He first laid hands on the blind man, Jesus asked him, "How do you see?" The man replied, "I can see now, but I don't see men as real men. I see men as trees walking."

"And he took the blind man by the hand, and led him out of the town... and (Jesus) put his hands upon him, he asked him if he saw ought (clearly). And he looked up, and said, I see men as trees, walking." Mark 8:23-24

Unfortunately, we live in a world where all men and women are not regarded as humans... real humans with equal rights and privileges. As with so many in the world today, the blind man saw men and women, but not as real human beings.

Nelson Mandela once said..."No one is born hating another person because of the color of his skin, or his background, or his religion. People must learn to hate, and if they can learn to hate, they can be taught to love."

A lot of misguided people in our society who have been taught to hate, see people as things, objects and sub-humans. African-Americans who set out to trace their ancestry, quickly discover that they can only go so far back through birth records.

At a certain point, to fully accomplish their goal they must switch from birth records to livestock deeds. Black men, women children weren't seen as humans, but livestock; animals... or trees walking.

In some cases, they were branded like the rest of the livestock. It was the belief of their masters that they weren't human enough to feel the branding iron.

In the case of the blind man, a second touch was required from the Master's hand. After laying hands on the man again, Jesus asked him, "Now, how do you see?" The man replied, "I see men as men!"

> *"After that, he put his hands again upon his eyes, and made him look up: and he was restored, and saw every man clearly."*
>
> Mark 8:25 (KJV)

"The world as we have known it... may be gone forever!"

Annese E. Jackson

Chapter Ten

"NECESSITY" IS THE MOTHER OF INVENTION

"Our World Is Changed Forever!"

Yes, the coronavirus left much death and destruction in its trail. But as odd as it may seem, there was also good that came from this tragedy. The good left behind by the pandemic is too vast to calculate. None of us will ever know all of the good things and wonderful things that came as a result of the COVID, but they are many.

As with most great discoveries, necessity mandates that we figure out a way to solve huge unanticipated problems. And of course, the novel coronavirus certainly introduced its own share of new problems and new or lesser familiar terms… like social distancing, shelter-at-home, zoonotic and "N-95" mask.

It also gave new meaning to the term "drive-by." Whereas previously, drive-by had a sad and deadly meaning. A drive-by used to bring fear and horror, as unsuspecting individuals are gunned down by cold-hearted shooters from a moving vehicle.

Because of the coronavirus, drive-by now means something far more enjoyable. People are now able to practice social-distancing while celebrating the birthday, anniversary, graduation or special event of a friend or loved one. This is done by driving past the home of the honoree, in a celebratory parade, honking horns and waving.

So, along with the N-95 facial mask, people have begun wearing full-face, see-through shields to protect them from coughs, sneezes, or intentional spitting.

A drone manufacturer claimed to have drones that could detect the virus from forty feet in the air. That would greatly assist medical professionals and first responders in testing potential COVID victims while maintaining social distancing.

I don't think anyone can deny that, after the coronavirus is long behind us, necessitated technology has forced a change in how we do things in the world today.

Video conferencing has brought the world into our living rooms. Whereas, you used to have to wake up and get dressed to go to work, many of you can now go into the office without getting out of bed. School teachers are teaching their classes from their home computers, and kids are going to class from their laptops.

Salesmen and saleswomen, who hate face-to-face or door-to-door sales, have discovered that they can now make a pretty decent living in sales, without having to visit with potential prospects. Not only is this a time-saver, but it is also a lot safer.

CHAPTER 10   "NECESSITY" IS THE MOTHER OF INVENTION

By the way, have you noticed how doctors are back to making house calls… but while still at their own house? Doctors are now able to visit with you, diagnose you, and submit prescriptions for you… all electronically! And, the pharmacist will fill the prescription and have it delivered to your door.

While quarantining and social-distancing, millions of people did all their shopping online; from groceries to auto parts. New clothes, piping hot meals and pet supplies are all obtainable without leaving home. Companies like Amazon, eBay and Walmart are now all being pushed beyond their limits.

And oh yeah, about those mega-churches, well some of those neighborhood churches that they forced into obscurity, are now on even playing ground. These days, any ministry can reach thousands of worshipers from home.

In conclusion, there are so many varying reasons given… and alleged divine revelations, on the truth behind the Novel Coronavirus. They can't all be true. But, I'll tell you one thing that is true—

"The world as we have known it… is gone forever!"

"A new commandment I give to you, that you love one another, even as I have loved you, that you also love one another. By this all men will know that you are My disciples, if you have love for one another."

John 13:34-35 (NASB)

— WHY WE WROTE THIS BOOK —

We wrote this book because people around me, and around the world have been frightened over the Novel Coronavirus pandemic.

The pandemic is real…and real people are dying every day. These are not actors, but real people! Hundreds of thousands have died. Many of the dead were Christian church leaders and church members.

They thought they were safe from the COVID, but the world has since discovered, the Coronavirus will (and has) strike down anyone, including church bishops and church congregates. Many people in the church are frightened beyond human imagination.

We wrote this book because so many within the church are asking if the church is being punished. Or, if the COVID was sent by God to purge the church of its wickedness, and its evil leaders. Some are calling it a cleansing of the pulpit. The church people are wanting answers. People everywhere are wanting answers.

We wrote this book because We hope to provide help, advice, encouragement and guidance for sincere believers who may be genuinely seeking help and direction regarding his or her own fears through a very dismal period.

We wrote this book because, We Care!

ABOUT THE AUTHORS

Bishop Frank Jackson, is the Chief Executive Director of the United Council of World Ministries. World-respected husband and father, Frank Jackson is appreciated for more than twenty active years in radio and TV broadcasting.

He is a former foreign missionary leader with a particular emphasis on short-term missionary projects in third world countries.

Both, directly and indirectly, he has trained pastors, Christian leaders, and church laity around the world. He has created hundreds of intense Bible study lessons and Christian training curriculum.

In sports, he has served as a staff chapel speaker to both the American League and National league professional major baseball teams.

As a founding director of Americans Resisting Minority & Ethnic Discrimination (ARMED), Bishop Jackson has traveled across America fighting against human and US Constitutional rights violations.

Frank Jackson is the author of the bestselling book, THUG PREACHERS (*The Unspoken Truth of Pastors Who Rule Through Fear, Bullying and Intimidation*).

fjackson@ucwministries.org

ABOUT THE AUTHORS
(Continued)

Pastor Annese E. Jackson, an internationally ordained minister, was born in Belize Central America. She is the Executive Administrator and Global Managing Director of the United Council of World Ministries (UCWM).

Annese Jackson, an honorably discharged United States soldier, who served through Desert Storm, is the holder of  two earned degrees from the University of Illinois, in the United States. She is the loving wife of Bishop Frank Jackson and the mother of five (four surviving) children.

For more than twenty years, she has established herself as a respected expert in non-profit organizations. Rev. Jackson, a very serious police accountability advocate, is the National Managing Director of Americans Resisting Minority & Ethnic Discrimination (ARMED).

As a true protector of Constitutional, civil and human rights, racial equality and equal justice for all people, Jackson goes before our government legislators, colleges and universities,... and the news media, to speak out against prison abuse, police violence, inhumane deportation, and the broken criminal justice system in America. She also an advocate of bail reform.

A long-standing home-schooling mother, Annese E. Jackson has been the national director of WISH (*Working to Inspire Students at Home*) Home-school Foundation for twelve years.

ajackson@ucwministries.org

Thank you for your support.

APPENDIX

Both, the authors and the publisher of "COVID-19 and the CHURCH" wish to acknowledge the significance of the following individuals, organizations and institutions in the research, development and production of this book.

Strong's Concordance with Hebrew and Greek Lexicon
http://lexiconcordance.com

Vine's Complete Expository Dictionary of Old and New Testament Wordshttp://www.ultimatebiblereferencelibrary.com/Vines_Expositary_Dictionary.pdf

Association for Diplomatic Studies and Training - http://adst.org

Dr. Chet Weld, Director of Pastoral Counseling at Casas Church
https://www.preachitteachit.org/about-us/the-team/chet-weld

Chicago Tribune - http://www.chicagotribune.com/news

Eugene Cho, co-founder and executive director of One Day's Wages
http://www.onedayswages.org/profile/eugene-cho

Eugene Cho, author of
Death by Ministry, Is pastoral ministry a dangerous profession
http://eugenecho.com/2010/08/11/death-by-ministry

APPENDIX

Kent R. Rieske, Ministry Director - Bible Life Ministry
http://www.biblelife.org

Dr. Joseph Mattera, Presiding Bishop of Christ Covenant Coalition and Overseeing Bishop of Resurrection Church in New York

Fast Facts about American Religion
http://hirr.hartsem.edu/research/fastfacts/fast_facts.html

Mike Fehlauer, Pastor, Author, Director of Foundation Ministries
The Christian Broadcasting Network (CBN)
http://www.cbn.com/partners/about/our-ministries

Goodreads quotes
http://www.goodreads.com

Hebrew Interlinear Bible (OT)
http://www.scripture4all.org/OnlineInterlinear/Hebrew_Index.htm

Greek Interlinear Bible (NT)
http://www.scripture4all.org/OnlineInterlinear/Greek_Index.htm

Weinstein's Federal Evidence, Second Edition
by Jack Weinstein, Margaret Berger, and Joseph M. McLaughlin

APPENDIX

The American Church in Crisis: Ground Breaking Research Based on a National Database of over 200,000 Churches by David T. Olson

What is Going on with the Pastors in America? by Dr. Richard J. Krejcir
http://www.intothyword.org/apps/articles/?articleid=36562

Toxic Faith by Stephen Arterburn

Twisted Scriptures by Mary Alice Chrnalogar

What was happening when 1984 was written?
https://study.com/academy/lesson/when-was-1984-written.html

When Was 1984 Written? | Study.com
study.com › academy › lesson › when-was-1984-written

About Microbiology – Viruses
microbiologyonline.org › introducing-microbes › viruses

Virus Structure <Generally, all virus have certain common components.>   https://msu.edu/course/mmg/569/Virus%20Structure.htm

About Microbiology – Viruses
microbiologyonline.org › introducing-microbes › viruses

APPENDIX

What Are Viruses?
https://www.livescience.com/53272-what-is-a-virus.html
Aparna Vidyasagar - Live Science Contributor

Merriam Webster:
https://www.merriam.webster.com/dictionary/collateral%20damage?utm_campaign=sd&utm_medium=serp&utm_source=jsonld

https://www.thesaurus.com/

https://www.dictionary.com/

When our heroes fall © Ronald P. Hutchcraft 2019
https://harrisondaily.com/free/when-our-heroes-fall/article_5acc6a0e-c429-11e9-ae55-aff5eef8a09f.html

10 Types of Biblical Suffering
https://midtowncolumbia.com/blog/10-types-of-suffering
Midtown Fellowship
Pastor Jon Ludovina and teaching team resident Garrison Weiner

Suzie Eller
https://proverbs31.org/read/devotions/full-post/2013/02/15/collateral-damage

APPENDIX

THUG PREACHERS
"The Unspoken Truth of Pastors
Who Rule Through Fear, Bullying and Intimidation"
thugpreachers.com
xavierpublishinghouse.com

The rightwing Christian preachers in deep
denial over the COVID's danger
https://www.theguardian.com/us-news/2020/apr/04/america-rightwing-christian-preachers-virus-hoax
Jason Wilson @jason_a_w

Pastors are supporting Trump in this health dilemma:
#Trump #Coronavirus #News / Now This News
https://youtu.be/AQUcxQwqT7w

Conservative Pastors Encourage Congregants
to Dismiss the COVID |
Now This News
https://youtu.be/Z200D8dAWLM

A pastor is receiving criticism for hold services
despite the coronavirus outbreak,
KDKA's Ross Guidotti reports

https://youtu.be/yJ9x9jyDXDI

https://youtu.be/gG66OhDO-as

APPENDIX

CNN / CNN
CNN's Victor Blackwell/Tony Spell interview
How can you be pro-life and keep your church open?
https://youtu.be/0FSq8J8Ixek

MSNBC anchor Ari Melber.
Deadly': Pelosi Says Trump's
Coronavirus Failures Cost American Lives | MSNBC
https://youtu.be/PVz1xfPQEio

http://on.msnbc.com/Instamsnbc
'Deadly': Pelosi Says Trump's Coronavirus Failures Cost American Lives | MSNBC

General Characteristics of Viruses
SUMMARY GENERAL CHARACTERISTICS OF VIRUSES
https://www.sparknotes.com/biology/microorganisms/viruses/section1/
By Bryan Walsh

Centers for Disease Control (CDC)
https://www.cdc.gov/coronavirus/2019-ncov/index.html

Christian Pastor Claims Coronavirus Is God's 'Death Angel
https://youtu.be/kHBZpl_CObY

APPENDIX

Live Science
6 in 10 Infectious Diseases Come from Animals.
By Yasemin Saplakogluhttps://www.livescience.com/65417-top-concerning-zoonotic-diseases.html

Jim and Tammy Faye Bakker
https://en.wikipedia.org/wiki/Jim_Bakker

Jim Bakker
https://www.history.com/this-day-in-history/jim-bakker-is-indicted-on-federal-charges

OJ Simpson
https://www.tvguide.com/celebrities/oj-simpson/credits/168428/

https://en.wikipedia.org/wiki/O._J._Simpson

The Word Walk: Pandemic and The Bible
Rafael Bastien-Herrera

https://hanfordsentinel.com/community/selma_enterprise/opinion/the-word-walk-pandemic-and-the-bible/article_ee8f1f25-b130-51c3-ac7d-69d78b4691f6.html

Christianity Today
christianitytoday.com

APPENDIX

Five-Fold Ministry
https://www.fivefoldministry.com/static/
learn-about-the-five-fold-ministry
Created by Eric Knopf
Eric@Visionlaunchers.com)

McCormick Place medical facility to wind down, as the COVID slows
https://www.chicagotribune.com/coronavirus/ct-coronavirus-mccormick-place-shutting-down-20200501-7k7eltzswbf2njbht6utyabn6q-story.html

The National Guard and Army Corps of Engineers
https://abc7chicago.com/coronavirus-illinois-cases-update-national-guard/6062180/

https://www.healthline.com/health/worst-disease-outbreaks-history#15

God, "Why Have You Made Me Your Target"? (Job 7:20)
Mark Banschick M.D. psychologytoday.com

National Catholic Reporter
https://www.ncronline.org/news/vatican/the
COVID-not-gods-judgment-call-live-differently-
Cindy Wooden, Catholic News Service

RESOURCES

THUG PREACHERS
thugpreachers.com

Xavier Publishing House
xavierpublishinghouse.com

STUDY.COM
study.com

Michigan State University
https://msu.edu

Live Science
https://www.livescience.com

Merriam Webster Dictionary
merriam-webster.com

Online Thesaurus
https://www.thesaurus.com/

Online Dictionary
https://harrisondaily.com

RESOURCES

Proverbs 31 Ministries
https://proverbs31.org

National catholic Reporter
https://www.ncronline.org/news

The Guardian News Source
https://www.theguardian.com

Now This News
https://nowthisnews.com

CNN News
CNN.com

MSNBC
http://on.msnbc.com/Instamsnbc

#international #news #newsreporterdancing
https://youtu.be/kHBZpl_CObY.com

Sparks Notes
https://www.sparknotes.com

RESOURCES

Christianity Today
christianitytoday.com

TV Guide
https://www.tvguide.com
   Hanford Sentinel
https://hanfordsentinel.com

Chicago Tribune
https://www.chicagotribune.com

ABC-TV Chicago
https://abc7chicago.com

Healthline
https://www.healthline.com

Wikipedia
https://en.wikipedia.org

Midtown Fellowship
https://midtowncolumbia.com

RESOURCES

Manners and Customs of Bible Lands
Book by Fred Hartley Wight
https://books.google.com/books/about/Manners_and_Customs_of_Bible_Lands.html?id=-y5kjwEACAAJ&source=kp_book_description

Five-Fold Ministry
https://www.fivefoldministry.com

NowThis NEWS
https://www.youtube.com/channel/UCn4sPeUomNGIr26bElVdDYg

INDEX

A

abused 49
acceptance 50
afflict 69
African-American 51
AIDS 62
aircraft 39
airplane 39
ATF 51
angels 54, 76
angel 28, 115
animal 61, 64, 93, 94
Apostle 33
Apostles 33
aquarium 33
arenas 35
Army Corps of Engineers 67, 117
Asaph 86
Asian Flu 62
assemblage 64
attachment 64
attack 42, 50, 51, 68, 69, 72, 75, 97
auditoriums 28, 32
author 8, 10, 42, 43, 44, 106, 110
authorities 65, 89, 93

B

Babylon 78
bacteria 61
Bakker. Jim 41, 116
Bakker, Tammie Faye 41
bats 93
bestselling book 95, 106
Bible 7, 20, 21, 27, 30, 34, 42, 73, 84, 85, 89, 106, 111, 116, 122

INDEX

Biblical 33, 113
birds 93
bishops 83
bitten 94
blasphemed 77, 78
blessed 10, 21, 22, 79, 86
blood 30, 72, 75, 76, 77, 79
bloodstream 95
bodies 19, 67, 68
bomb 50
bombing attack 42
bowl 76, 77, 78
Branch Davidian 51
Brazil 63
breakthroughs 99
breathing 98
brightness 25, 41
bright 25, 41
broken 43
bug 94
bugs 93
empire 29, 31

C

capsid 61, 64
carnage 68
casualties 48
catheters 96, 98
Center for Disease Control 93
religious celebrities 40
Center for Disease Control 93
characteristics 64
Chicago 34, 67, 68, 110, 121
child 49, 51, 52, 53, 69
childhood 49

INDEX

children 43
China 18, 57, 63
cholera 62
church 6, 8, 19, 23, 27, 28, 29, 30, 31, 32, 33, 34, 35, 36, 37, 40, 42, 43, 44, 47, 48, 81, 82, 83, 84, 85, 86, 105, 106, 115
church idols 42
civilian 48
clean 95
cleansing 48, 85, 105
Cleveland, Ohio 51, 53
CPD 51, 53
collateral damage 42, 48, 49, 51
Coming Attractions 75
command 74, 88
commandments 73
communicated 87
communicate 87
community 35, 52, 66, 116
compassion 19, 43
congregates 31, 84, 105
congregates 31, 84, 105
congregation 29, 32, 36
consequences 73, 99
contagious 37, 99
contaminated 94, 95, 98
contributors 86
Cook County 68
coronavirus 8, 17, 19, 22, 28, 36, 47, 57, 58, 62, 63, 64, 65, 67, 82, 83, 84, 88, 93, 96, 101, 102, 114, 115, 117
the COVID 8, 17, 19, 22, 28, 36, 47, 57, 58, 62, 63, 64, 65, 67, 82, 83, 84, 88, 93, 96, 101, 102, 114, 115, 117
corpse 76
coughs 62, 102
cremation 68
cure 20, 36, 59, 75

INDEX

D

darkness 24, 25, 77, 80, 87, 90
darkest 24
David Koresh 51
deadliest 59, 68
death 16, 18, 34, 55, 58, 61, 63, 64, 71, 73, 83, 85, 97, 98, 101, 110
deaths 6, 34, 40, 50, 59, 63, 71, 95, 96, 97, 98, 99
denominations 6, 48
disease 18, 28, 36, 58, 61, 65, 66, 67, 74, 80, 87, 90, 94, 96, 97, 98, 99, 117
deserve 20, 22
devastation 43
devour 74
dictionary 48, 113
die 83
diphtheria 62
disciples 74, 75, 104
discord 37
discoveries 101
infectious diseases 36
disobedience 73
doors 28, 81, 85, 87
Welds. Dr. Chet 43
Dr. Ignaz Semmelweis 98
drive-by 102
drone 102
Dr. Peter Pronovost 96, 97
dynasties 29

E

Egypt 72
Egyptians 73
emergency centers 67
empathize 20

INDEX

empathy 19, 20
empathy filter 19
empathy switch 19
personal empire 31
end-time 76, 82
enemy 68
envelope 61
epicenter 65, 66, 67
epidemic 62, 65, 66, 68
essential workers 82
Ethan 86
Evangelist 33
Evangelists 33, 34
executing 27, 47
executive orders 13, 63
executive security 53
exhales 62
exotic cars 29
Ezrahite 86

F

faith 13, 19, 25, 28, 33, 44, 87, 88
fallen soldiers 41
fallout 44
family dynasty 29, 31
famine 75, 82
FBI 51
finisher 44
first family 30
first responders 82, 96, 102
fish 32
fishers 32
fishing 32, 33
five-fold ministry 33
follow 32, 43

INDEX

friends 23
full-gospel 33
funeral homes 68

G

glass ceiling 31
gloves 95
gospel 33, 74, 89
government officials 65
Great Commission 32
greedy dogs 30
grief 21, 68
gun 51, 52
gun-wielding 52

H

hands 52, 53, 59, 72, 89, 94, 95, 98
hardship 89
heal 74
healing 74, 75
healthcare 82, 96, 97
heaven 74, 75, 77, 78
Heman 86
heroes 96, 113 HIV 62
holiness 33
hospital 67, 94, 95, 96, 97, 98
host 61, 64, 71, 86
host body. 61
host cells 61
hotspot 65, 66
hotspots 94
household 43
Hubei 18, 57
humanity 6, 28, 78
human remains 68

INDEX

human 93
hurt 19, 42, 44, 48, 49
suffering 18, 19, 20, 21, 22, 23, 24, 28, 69, 85, 89, 113

I

idols 40, 42, 44
Illinois 67, 107
illness 21
image 76
impact 43
incidental 29, 48
infected 37, 58, 62, 63, 64, 94
influenza 62
innocent 42, 43, 50, 53
integrity 22, 85
intended target 48
Iran 63
Italy, 63

J

JB Pritzker, Governor 67
jets 29
Jimmy Swaggert 41
Job 20, 21, 22, 23, 24, 117
judgment 7, 27, 53, 76, 117
justice 20

K

children 13, 18, 24, 43, 49, 50, 51, 53, 87, 107
kids 49, 102
Koresh, David 86
Kingdom 29, 31, 32, 33, 34
Kingdom Building 32, 33, 34
Michael Jackson 41
King Solomon 25

INDEX

L

Lazarus 88
leader 43
leaders 6, 28, 29, 32, 34, 41, 42, 43, 44, 47, 63, 84, 88, 105, 106
Lightfoot, Mayor Lori
lightning 78
neighborhood 35, 51, 103
locusts 74
Loehmann, Officer Timothy 51, 52
love 13, 21, 23, 30, 49, 72, 73, 104

M

mall 35
mansions 29
mass graves 68
mass panic 65
Mayor Lori Lightfoot 67
McCormick Place 67, 117
measles 62
meat 94
medical 20, 96, 102
medical spokespersons 65
medications 94, 95
medicine 94
mega-church 36, 42
members 6, 9, 28, 30, 31, 32, 34, 36, 37, 43, 47, 82, 83, 84, 98, 105
merciful 73
Merriam Webster 48, 113, 118
message 87
message 87
millionaires 29
miracle 88
miracles 74, 88
misery 19, 58, 68

INDEX

missile 56, 68, 69
mission 76
mock hospital rooms 67
monetary 28, 30, 31
moral 42
morgue 68
Moses 86
most lethal 62
Mount Carmel Church 51
Murrah Federal Building 50

N

mask 102
National Guard 67, 117
Native American 62
necessity 101
neighborhood 35, 51, 103
New Testament 32, 72, 74, 75, 110
Nicole Brown Simpson 40
non-compliance 83
nurses 81, 94, 95

O

obey 73, 88
officer 51, 52, 53, 107
Oklahoma City 50
Old Testament 22, 30, 72, 86
opposition 25
oppressed 87
oppressors 87
O.J. Simpson 40
outbreak 61, 62, 68, 71, 99, 117

INDEX

P

pandemic 6, 8, 19, 20, 23, 24, 28, 47, 48, 58, 59, 62, 63, 64, 65, 66, 67, 68, 69, 71, 76, 78, 83, 84, 88, 93, 99, 101, 105, 116
pandemics 7, 21, 65, 72, 75, 76, 78, 84
parishioners 9, 28, 84
particles 64
Pastors 28, 31, 33, 34, 83, 95, 106, 112, 114, 118
penetration 64
Pentagon 51
pentecostal 42
pestilence 72, 74
pigs 93
plague 72, 73, 75, 78, 87
PLT Club 41
polio 62
positive 25
power 20, 24, 69, 72, 74, 75, 88
preachers 3, 23, 32, 82, 96
Preckwinkle, Toni 68
Pritzker, Governor JB 67
professionals 11, 20, 64, 82, 96, 102
promise 54, 87
prophesying 75
Prophet 33
Prophets 33
proselytizing 31
prosperity 21
hedge 85
scholars 85
psalmist 87, 90
pseudo-ownership 30
psychopathic 19
pulpit 48, 105
punishment 20, 21, 23, 27, 73
purging 48

145

INDEX

Q

quarantine 63, 83, 85, 88, 89
quarantining 90, 103

R

rain 74, 75
rats 93
Suarez 97
refrigerated 68
release 64, 76
religious 6, 23, 40, 41, 42, 44, 69, 84
Reno, Janet 51
repentance 73
reproduction 64
research 8, 11, 18, 20, 110, 111
respecter of person 47
restoration 73
revival 33
revivals 33
wash 95, 98
ripple effect 43
risk 13, 28, 63, 82, 84
Robert Tilton 41
rock stars 40
Ron Goldman 40

S

sanctuaries 28
sanitary 95
Satan 22, 24
scarlet fever 62
science 99
scientific authorities 65

INDEX

scientist 20
Scott Bradley 34
secretly 87
Secret Service 53
self-esteem 49
self-worth 49
September 11 50
sermon 37
services 8, 28, 31, 36, 84, 114
seven angels 76
seven bowls 76
shelter-in-place 63
shields 102
shining 25, 42
sin 22, 32, 43, 74, 76, 79
sins 27, 28, 50, 73, 79
skeleton crew 84
sky 75
Smallpox 62
sneezes 62, 102
social-distancing 63, 102
Solomon 25, 74, 86
Swaggert, Jimmy 41
Korah 86
sorrow 68
lost souls 32, 33
Spain 63
Spanish flu 62
spanked 49
Spirit-filled 33
spiritual warfare 42
stadiums 28, 35, 99
status 30, 47, 69
statutes 73
stories 9, 41, 87

INDEX

strength 25, 86, 87
stripes 79
suffering 18, 19, 20, 21, 22, 23, 24, 28, 69, 85, 89, 113
sunshine 25
Swine flu 62
synagogues 74

T

Tamir 51, 52
Tamir Rice 51
Tammie Faye 41
Tammie Faye Bakker 41
Tammie Faye Messner 41
Teachers 33
Teacher 33
technology 31, 102
televangelism 41
televangelists 41
television 98
terminology 65
terrorism by litigation 54
terrorist attack 50, 97
terror 80, 87
Terry Nichols 50
therapist 43
THUG PREACHERS 6, 29, 95, 106, 114, 118
officer Loehmann 52
Timothy Loehmann 51
Timothy McVeigh 50
tomb 88
Toni Preckwinkle 68
touch 74, 80, 90, 95
transgressions 23, 79
treat 95
trials 21, 25, 89

INDEX

tribulations 21
Donald J Trump 63
typhoid fever 62

U

unchurched 47
unclean spirits 74, 77
uncoating 64
United States 4, 9, 63, 137
unpreserved 94
unrefrigerated 94
unsanitary 94, 97
untested 24, 94
urine 95
U.S. Attorney General 51

V

conferencing 102
virus 18, 57, 61, 62, 63, 64, 68, 69, 82, 83, 84, 88, 94, 102, 112, 113, 114

W

Waco Texas 53
war 48, 86
warehouse 68
warfare 42
weapon 52, 53, 68
West Africa 62
the World Health Organization 58, 66
pertussis 62
two (2) witnesses 75
witnesses 75
World Trade Center 50
worship 28, 84
wounded 79
Wuhan 18, 57

INDEX

Y
yachts 29
yellow fever, 62

Z
zoonotic 93, 94, 102, 116

COVID-19 and the CHURCH
by FRANK AND ANNESE JACKSON

2020 © XAVIER PUBLISHING HOUSE, INC®
Published and Printed in the United States of America
All Rights Reserved

www.ingramcontent.com/pod-product-compliance
Lightning Source LLC
Chambersburg PA
CBHW031645040426
42453CB00006B/211